MACMILLAN MODERN DRAMA

Macmillan Modern Dramatists

Series Editors: *Bruce King* and *Adele King*

Reed Anderson, *Federico Garcia Lorca*
Eugene Benson, *J. M. Synge*
Renate Benson, *German Expressionist Drama*
Normand Berlin, *Eugene O'Neill*
Michael Billington, *Alan Ayckbourn*
Roger Boxill, *Tennessee Williams*
John Bull, *New British Political Dramatists*
Dennis Carroll, *David Mamet*
Neil Carson, *Arthur Miller*
Maurice Charney, *Joe Orton*
Ruby Cohn, *New American Dramatists, 1960–1980*
Bernard F. Dukore, *American Dramatists, 1918–1945*
Bernard F. Dukore, *Harold Pinter*
Arthur Ganz, *George Bernard Shaw*
James Gibbs, *Wole Soyinka*
Frances Gray, *John Arden*
Frances Gray, *Noel Coward*
Charles Hayter, *W. S. Gilbert and Arthur Sullivan*
Julian Hilton, *Georg Büchner*
David Hirst, *Edward Bond*
Helene Keyssar, *Feminist Theatre*
Bettina L. Knapp, *French Theatre 1918–1939*
Charles Lyons, *Samuel Beckett*
Gerry McCarthy, *Edward Albee*
Jan McDonald, *The 'New Drama' 1900–1914*
Susan Bassnett-McGuire, *Luigi Pirandello*
Margery Morgan, *August Strindberg*
Leonard C. Pronko, *Eugene Labiche and Georges Feydeau*
Jeanette L. Savona, *Jean Genet*
Claude Schumacher, *Alfred Jarry and Guillaume Apollinaire*
Laurence Senelick, *Anton Chekhov*
Theodore Shank, *American Alternative Theatre*
James Simmons, *Sean O'Casey*
Ronald Speirs, *Bertolt Brecht*
David Thomas, *Henrick Ibsen*
Dennis Walder, *Athol Fugard*
Thomas Whitaker, *Tom Stoppard*
Nick Worrall, *Nikolai Gogol and Ivan Turgenev*
Katharine Worth, *Oscar Wilde*

Further titles in preparation

MACMILLAN MODERN DRAMATISTS

NOEL COWARD

Frances Gray
Lecturer in English Literature
University of Sheffield

MACMILLAN

For Emily

First published 1987

Published by
Higher and Further Education Division
MACMILLAN PUBLISHERS LTD
Houndmills, Basingstoke, Hampshire RG21 2XS
and London
Companies and representatives
throughout the world

Typeset by Wessex Typesetters
(Division of The Eastern Press Ltd)
Frome, Somerset

Printed in Hong Kong

British Library Cataloguing in Publication Data
Gray, Frances
Noel Coward.—(Macmillan modern dramatists)
1. Coward, Nöel—Criticism and
interpretation
I. Title
822'.912   PR6005.085Z/
ISBN 0–333–29332–0
ISBN 0–333–29333–9 Pbk

Contents

List of Plates

Acknowledgements

I should like to thank the University of Sheffield Research Fund for a grant to write this book; Christina Katíc for help with the typescript; Joe Mitchenson for access to so much valuable material and for his patience in guiding me through it.

The publishers and I wish to thank the following who have kindly given permission for the use of copyright material: Associated Book Publishers (UK) Ltd. for extracts from *Private Lives* by Noel Coward and for various songs from *Noel Coward Songbook*, Methuen London.

The BBC Hulton Picture Library, Mander and Mitchenson, and Sotheby's for photographs.

Every effort has been made to trace all the copyright holders but if any have been inadvertently overlooked the publishers will be pleased to make the necessary arrangement at the first opportunity.

Editors' Preface

The *Macmillan Modern Dramatists* is an international series of introductions to major and significant nineteenth and twentieth-century dramatists, movements and new forms of drama in Europe, Great Britain, America and new nations such as Nigeria and Trinidad. Besides new studies of great influential dramatists of the past, the series includes volumes on contemporary authors, recent trends in the theatre and on many dramatists, such as writers of farce, who have created theatre 'classics' while being neglected by literary criticism. The volumes in the series devoted to individual dramatists include a biography, a survey of the plays, and detailed analysis of the most significant plays, along with discussion, where relevant, of the political, social, historical and theatrical context. The authors of the volumes, who are involved with theatre as playwrights, directors, actors, teachers and critics, are concerned with the plays as theatre and discuss such matters as performance, character interpretation and staging, along with themes and contexts.

BRUCE KING

ADELE KING

1
The Mask

Once, he showed us how the mask was made. In 1935 Noel Coward was broke after the failure of his mildly experimental play *Point Valaine*. It prompted him to take on his first starring role in a movie, Hecht and MacArthur's *The Scoundrel*. Despite its low-budget status, this rapidly became something of a cult film, largely because of its intelligent exploitation of the persona which Coward had spent his life in polishing. Tony Mallare, the Scoundrel, was a simplified version of the Coward charm – a charm which gained intensity by the easy impudence with which it revealed its own artifice. In a memorable opening sequence, Coward constructed him for us piece by piece in front of the camera.

You hear the voice first: clipped, reedy, precise, firing epigrams from behind a shower-curtain. Then the body appears: naked, sleek as an otter, slim to the point of weediness in an era whose idea was the broad-shouldered butch of Clark Gable. As soon as he is decent enough for the censor, Coward turns to the props that the image requires: the tie is elaborately knotted, the hair groomed to within an inch of its life; the functional parts of his costume, the shoes and jacket, can wait; but he needs a drink and a cigarette with which to complete himself. And while the process of dandification takes place, he goes on delivering epigrams at machine-gun speed, dividing them equally between his hangers-on and, with a self-mocking bow, his mirror. He is everlastingly framed, Tony Mallare, in doorways, in windows, always making a conscious artefact of himself.

Even while we see the process, we are of course aware that it is inimitable. When the conjuror is naked it is only to prove that he can still produce something from up a ghostly sleeve. But, tailor-made for Coward, the part of Tony Mallare satisfyingly encapsulates the Coward image and even symbolically foreshadows its future career. For Mallare may be a scoundrel, with a thrilling reputation for wickedness, but he does nothing that would shock your great-aunt. He entices a young poetess away from her blustering failure of a fiancé (who promptly tries both murder and suicide) and he refuses to publish a bad manuscript out of compassion for the author's family problems – actions which have at least some claim to integrity. Nonetheless, when Mallare drowns on his way to do a little philandering abroad, a spectral voice sends his ghost back to obtain the tears of a loving heart to save him from eternal damnation. Coward plays all this to the hilt, no sign of tongue in cheek even for his final, immaculately moral assumption into heaven to the strains of Rachmaninov.

He himself did not have to die to attain this kind of respectability. Long before his memorial was erected in Westminster Abbey (near, but not in, Poet's Corner) he had become a knight and a national institution. Like Tony

Mallare, he had started with a reputation for 'wickedness', but all he did in fact was to project a persona which gave his audience an agreeable *frisson*. In the twenties, as he wrote in his introduction to *Play Parade One*, 'I was seldom mentioned in the press without allusions to cocktails, decadence and post-war hysteria.'[1] But although he portrayed such things onstage, his private life was orderly, reticent and without scandal; this, of course, permitted the audience to enjoy the persona with a clear conscience. When they responded, with giddy adulation or enjoyable outrage, to the name 'Noel Coward', they were responding not to a man but to a myth which combined the forbidden with the very safe, to a mixture of charm and hard work.

The myth is a potent and durable one. Coward's name has been useful to the advertising industry, and used to sell a range of items from razor blades to the QE2. His image has provided a convenient shorthand for a certain style. In his last film appearance, for example, in Otto Preminger's *The Italian Job*, Coward had a tiny role but everyone understood the character: as soon as he appeared in prison in an elegant dressing gown he symbolised the juxtaposition of the two values the film was juggling – law and order on the one hand, and on the other a sophisticated anarchy which still respected solid bourgeois values like the Royal Family.

The dressing gown was, of course, a Coward trademark, a metonym for the man and his aura. It has even been enshrined in a New York museum. Its place there speaks volumes about the difference between Coward and the majority of playwrights – whether greater or lesser. For our response to bits of their intimate *débris* is usually quite different. It is very moving, for example, to see Chekhov's dressing gown and slippers at Yalta, because they bring home the truth of mortality, the fact that although the plays live on the man is lost to us. It is no more moving to see Coward's dressing gown than it is to see the first Model-T Ford; for it does not suggest a man, a life, something in the past, but a style, a way of speaking and moving and timing laughs on stage which is, thanks to the plays, endlessly recapturable – in short, the Coward myth.

The myth has tended to get in the way of many critical studies of Coward. It contributes to a difficulty many scholars seem to feel in 'placing' him and his work. He is hard to ignore. In writing this book I spent a considerable amount of time in tracking his name through the indices of countless books – diaries, social histories, biographies of people from numerous walks of life; a surprising number of novels made use of his name to provide a bit of period flavour or as a touchstone for sophistication; one, which had better remain anonymous, summed up its decadent villain in the words 'a personal friend of Noel Coward.'

At the same time he is hard to classify. Many literary historians, although content to deal with novelists of no very great merit – Hugh Walpole, say – dismiss Coward as an 'entertainer' and evade a detailed examination of his plays by pointing out that on the page, as opposed to in performance, they are very thin indeed. Theatre historians have another kind of difficulty. Coward's work varies enormously in merit; some of his plays – perhaps even the majority – are thin and tedious in the extreme and prompted a host of imitations that were even more tedious. At certain stages in the history of the theatre – the late fifties in particular – the name 'Noel Coward' stood for all that was bad in English drama. At the same time, Coward was an acknowledged influence on writers of the stature of Pinter and Orton and was the author of five of the most enduring comedies of the century. These he identified himself in 1958:

To quote Madame Arcati, 'It came to me in a 'blinding flash' that I had written several important plays – *Hay Fever*, *Private Lives*, *Design for Living*, *Present Laughter* and *Blithe Spirit* . . . They mirrored, without over-exaggeration, a certain section of the social life of the times and, on re-reading them, I find them both unpretentious and well-constructed.[2]

He was, at his best, a writer of unnerving fluency: all five were written at high speed – *Private Lives* in four days – so that, in a sense, the critic dealing with the enduring work of Coward is concerned with about six weeks' work out of a lifetime of more than seventy years. But any attempt to examine these plays without some understanding of the Coward myth as a whole is doomed to failure. For the relationship between the mask of the player and the world as his audience is precisely their subject. It is possible to look at the plays without any knowledge of Coward's private life. He kept this very much to himself: even his autobiographies and published diaries give little away about his personal feelings – although they do indicate that he deliberately chose to ignore certain aspects of his own experience in his writing; he describes vividly, for instance, the violence of a nervous breakdown and the fear he felt when thought to have a brain tumour, but did not make direct use of it in his plays. It is possible to look at them without much reference to the major literary figures of his lifetime. Modernism, for instance, meant nothing to him; Joyce might as well not have existed and Beckett he regarded with baffled distaste. If he read the thirties poets, they only provided something for his instinctive conservatism to react against. He admired Shaw in his youth, but when, after reading *The Young Idea*, Shaw sensibly advised him 'Never . . . see or read my plays . . . get clean away from me'[3] Coward took the hint. He was a popular writer, a popular entertainer, using well-tried formulae rather than making innovations. He courted the public, not the critics. But you have only to look at *Private Lives* or *Hay Fever* alongside some of the best-sellers of Coward's youth – for instance, that bit of quintessentially 'twenties' drivel, *The Green Hat* – to see their lasting energy and quality, and to see that they spring from a profound concern with the relationship between the world and the popular entertainer's public mask.

The exact nature of the mask has proved hard to define. Critics have talked of wit, of charm, of sophistication and cleverness: but, in English, something faintly pejorative has always clung to these words; often they are accompanied by words like 'false' and 'phoney' and an air of suspicion tends to be tacitly there even when they are not. One of the earliest academic studies of Coward, for instance, even while comparing him (not unfavourably) with Congreve and Sheridan, remarked that 'In these plays is reflected Mr Coward's own set, a society whose members are all as clever as he.'[4] The word seems double-edged, implying perhaps as a corollary 'and they're not as clever as they think they are'.

In the most recent, and in many ways the most thoughtful, critical appraisal of Coward, John Lahr chooses for the Coward mask the word most often on Coward's own lips: charm. Charm is the power to attract, literally to cast a spell; but a charm also protects its wearer, implying vulnerability. The word 'charm', incidentally, is used to denote a precise unit of measurement in nuclear physics, and it would be as well to bear this precision in mind when applying it to Coward. In a study of his plays and their relationship to the public persona, 'charm' is not a vague word suggesting agreeable but rather specious attraction, but virtually a technical term.

'One's real inside self is a private place and should always stay like that', Coward told the *New York Times* in old age, but adding, 'I have taken a lot of trouble with my public face.'[5] He was concerned, indeed, with the smallest details of it, as his advice to Cecil Beaton showed:

Coward showed more aplomb, investigating me out of a detached curiosity . . . my walk was said to be undulating, my clothes too conspicuously exaggerated . . . 'We've been absolutely beastly to you', he admitted, 'But you've shown spirit and let's hope you've learned a lesson. It is important not to let the public have a loophole to lampoon you.' That, he explained, was why he studied his own facade. Now take his voice: it was definite, harsh, rugged. He stood firmly and solidly, dressed quietly . . . 'You should appraise yourself,' he went on, 'Your sleeves are too tight, your voice is too high and too precise. You mustn't do it. It closes so many doors. It limits you unnecessarily and young men with half your intelligence will laugh at you.' He shook his head and wrinkled his forehead and added disarmingly 'It's hard, I know. One would like to indulge one's own taste . . . I take ruthless stock of myself in the mirror before going out. A polo jumper or unfortunate tie exposes one to danger.' He cocked one eye at me in mockery.[6]

The mockery and the sense of danger were equally real. Coward liked to puncture the various images of him created by the press. To the assertion that *Fallen Angels* was obscene he replied that 'The realisation that I am hopelessly depraved, vicious and decadent has for two days ruined my morning beaker of opium.'[7] To anyone who fancied him as the romantic creator of *Bitter-Sweet* he pointed out in *Present Indicative* that it was written while he was recovering from an operation for piles. But if he enjoyed the comic aspects of the public mask he was also resentful of any suggestion that it was shallow, facile or lacking in intellectual energy. When Churchill responded to his desire to do some useful war-work with 'Go and sing to them when the guns are firing – that's your job!' Coward was acid:

> With, I think, commendable restraint, I bit back the retort that if the morale of the Royal Navy was at such low ebb that the troops were unable to go into action without my singing 'Mad dogs and Englishmen' to them we were in trouble at the outset and that, although theoretically 'singing when the guns are firing' sounds extremely gallant it is, in reality, impracticable, because during a naval battle all ship's companies are at action stations, and the only place for me to sing would be in the ward-room by myself.[8]

Coward was fiercely, even naively, patriotic and the disappointment was genuine. So was his irritation at Churchill's unthinking acceptance of a showbiz cliché, his inability to distinguish between the easy charm of the mask and the intelligence it took to create it.

Churchill was by no means alone in this. The phrase on Coward's memorial – also the title of an excellent biography by Sheridan Morley – is one of Coward's own making: 'A talent to amuse', and it is frequently used to describe his special quality. But Coward did not originally say it of himself, and in its context its connotations are more complex than just a handy label. In occurs in *Bitter-Sweet*, in a song by the little café singer who is unlucky in love:

> I believe in doing what I can
> In crying when I must
> In laughing when I choose.
> Heigh-ho, if love were all
> I should be lonely,
> I believe the more you love a man,
> The more you give your trust,
> The more you're bound to lose.
> Although when shadows fall
> I think if only –
> Somebody splendid really needed me,
> Someone affectionate and dear,
> Cares would be ended if I knew that he
> Wanted to have me near.
> But I believe that since my life began
> The most I've had is just
> A talent to amuse.
> Heigho, if love were all!

Talent is not a quality possessed in a void; it is something which operates in a world of personal relationships and the betrayal and disillusionment that are an essential part of them. The variety of tensions between love and 'talent' is the backbone of the Coward charm, the source of its energy. Love, says the song, is not all – but nonetheless the central position of the word in the lyric asserts its importance. 'Talent' is the way the public persona operates in a world where love is chancy and dangerous.

AMANDA: What is so horrible is that one can't stay happy.
ELYOT: Darling, don't say that.

AMANDA: It's true. The whole business is a very poor joke.

ELYOT: Meaning that sacred and beautiful thing, Love?

AMANDA: Yes, meaning just that.

Coward's most famous and most passionate lovers are also the most uncompromising in their recognition that love comes to an end. Like Coward, they do not recognise any force greater than that of passion; if it fails, there is only one prop to lean on:

ELYOT: . . . Let's be superficial and pity the poor philosophers. Let's blow trumpets and squeakers, and enjoy the party as much as we can, like very small, quite idiotic school-children. Let's savour the delight of the moment. Come and kiss me darling, before your body rots, and worms pop in and out of your eye-sockets.

Any era of transition and decay, as Baudelaire observed, brings the dandy to the forefront of society. The dandy's commitment, like that of Elyot and Amanda, is primarily to style, to the marginal graces of living. He asserts that life is meaningless but that this is not particularly distressing. This stance requires a certain courage. To maintain it adequately one requires two things – first, the ability to blow the trumpets and squeakers properly; it is not easy to be a 'very small, quite idiotic child' without looking embarrassing and ungraceful when one has grown up; and second, one needs a private income with which to pay for them, or, at least, one cannot be *seen* to work. Dandies do not sweat. In Coward's best work we take this for granted; talent, and money, flow without obvious effort, and the harshness of the outside world does not intrude. Elyot and Amanda exist as though the Wall

Street crash had never happened; the unrepentant triangle in *Design For Living* might co-exist in time with the hunger marches of the thirties but they clearly inhabit a different universe. Bombs fell during the first run of *Blithe Spirit* but Elvira has died of laughter at a BBC broadcast.

This detachment can only be achieved by total self-absorption and, viewed in the light of day, Coward's characters are often, as John Lahr puts it, 'Monsters of vanity and selfishness.'[9] Only one thing prevents the plays from being morally repellent, and that is the exhilaration of the risk that the dandy's stance entails. The characters remain tolerable only as long as the wit flows and the talent flashes. To watch a performance of a Coward play is like watching a tightrope walker. And, in the best plays, the characters keep precariously balanced on their own charm and entertain us with their courage.

The cost of falling off was something Coward well understood. *The Vortex* showed two people whose grasp was less secure, trying to remain in the enchanted circle of charm by artificial aids – cocaine for Nicky, a young, dim, and ultimately unfaithful lover for Florence – and, in the end, losing their own peace of mind. *Easy Virtue* looked at the plight of charm and intelligence cast into the depths of second-rate county society with nothing to nourish it. Often, inevitably, Coward fell off his own tightrope. When he tried to introduce his irresponsibly charming characters into a real world, as he did in his comedy of race relations and colonial independence, *South Sea Bubble*, the wit became archness and the charm was coy. When he tried to be flippant about subjects of which he knew little, like modern painting in *Nude with Violin*, the joke fell flat. And sometimes, disastrously, he deserted the tightrope and tried to write with passion unleavened by wit. Whether the passion was erotic – as in *Point Valaine* – or political – as in *Post Mortem* – the results were shrill, lacking the energy which which he charged his frivolity to such effect. The tightrope was his only true natural habitat.

It was a dangerous place. For it meant that, until he finally achieved the status of Grand Old Man – the British are known for their affection for survivors – his relationship with the public was grounded on charm rather than on love. He had the entrepreneur's ability to gauge the public's desires and give them what they wanted before they knew they did, jumping adroitly from the shocks of *The Vortex* to the sentimentality of *Bitter-Sweet*, bringing on the whole company to sing *God Save the King* in *Cavalcade* and providing the audience with the cosy reassurance that it was 'still a pretty exciting thing to be English.' But the price of such self-proclaiming virtuosity was the unwillingness of his admiring audience to forgive failure.

Coward was a star, and the nature of his stardom was virtually unique. A star necessarily incarnates the capitalist belief in the individual, but the quality of the individuality was beginning to change. In Edwardian England the status of a beloved personality was in his or her own hands and those of a few agents and entrepreneurs. Figures like Lily Elsie and Charles Hawtrey were held in great affection, rather like specially talented members of the family. As the movies came to prominence, however, the stars began to lose their autonomy to the Hollywood machine. The movie star, in Walter Benjamin's words, 'preserves not the unique aura of the person but the "spell of the personality."'[10] In other words he is estranged from himself, his personality in the hands of the movie makers; he does not woo the audience himself but through them. The stars of the twenties and thirties attracted huge followings of passionate admirers, but their appeal was less homely, more paradoxical, than that of the Edwardian actors. They were more remote, more glamorous and unattainable: but on the other hand they were disseminated by the most popular medium in history, appearing in the local fleapits at the touch of a projection switch. Movie moguls, aware of this, treated them as public property; they had no private lives and were as exploitable off screen as on.

Coward uniquely combined these two aspects. He certainly attracted a cult following; even his early plays drew devotees heralding quite commonplace lines with 'Another Noelism'. Although he made relatively few appearances on film he managed to keep firmly in the public eye, through writing, acting, directing, through plays, stories, *bons mots* and frequent appearances in gossip columns. But he remained, more than any Hollywood star, in charge of his own fate, and this, perhaps, alienated him from his public as often as it drew their adulation. On the one hand, every young man of the twenties and thirties wanted to be Noel Coward. On the other, they could react with hysterical violence when the Noel Coward they saw was not the Noel Coward they wanted to be. After the first night of *Sirocco* – not a good play by any means, but no worse than many of its contemporaries – people spat on Coward as he left the theatre.

It was perhaps a reaction to the naked ambition that sometimes eclipsed the charm. While the habitual Coward mask was deceptively relaxed and effortless, he occasionally made it apparent that he was a self-made man and proud of it. Looking back over some early, rather glamorous, photographs of himself, he wrote

My face was plumper and less lined than it is now, and my figure was good but a bit weedy. Of what was going on inside me, however, there is no indication. There seems an emptiness somewhere and a blandness of expression in the eyes. There is little aggressiveness in the arranged smiles and no impatience apparent at all, and in this the camera must have lied . . .[11]

Although *The Vortex* established his reputation as the scourge of twenties 'Society', he wanted to gatecrash 'Society' himself. *Present Indicative* listed thirty-six famous names he had managed to meet in his early career. His portrayals of his own social stratum were different. He liked to flaunt his lower-middle-class origins and wrote himself several parts as suburban *paterfamilias* in plays like *This Happy Breed*. The assumption underlying these plays was the impossibility of social mobility. Frank Gibbons's daughter, for instance, gets 'above herself' and ends up in trouble, crawling back defeated to the bosom of the family. The plays portrayed a class system which had fixed boundaries – fixed, of course, to everybody but Coward himself, with his exceptional talent. This aggressively upward mobility attracted considerable flak; for instance, Coward's departure into tax exile drew hoots of derision from a press that had countenanced similar behaviour from others as rich and famous without a murmur.

His best work took for granted the primacy of talent and charm; it also adroitly allowed the audience into the talentocracy. Monstrously selfish his leading characters might be, but Coward seduced his audience into laughing with them and at the untalented, and so drew them into a flattering conspiracy. With a flourish, he revealed the inner workings of charm, the relationship between performer and mask. Sometimes the overtones were comic, inviting the audience to share the enjoyment of playing a role. Judith Bliss, for instance, in *Hay Fever*, smugly reflects that her beef-witted admirer loves not her but her 'Celebrated Actress Glamour'. Sometimes he invited rueful commiseration, as when Garry Essendine in *Present Laughter* complains that he is 'always watching myself go by' and is acting even as he speaks. When Coward played one of his own charmers the effect was intensified. He was not the kind of actor to sink his own identity in a part. He excelled in the intimacy of revue and made a new career for himself as a cabaret entertainer when his work fell out of favour in the fifties. While he did not stand back from his role and invite the cool judgement of the audience as a Brechtian actor might, he kept a slight distance from it in order to allow them to enjoy the process of creation; he enticed them not simply to laugh with him and find him attractive, but to share in the continuing creation of a myth called 'Noel Coward,' to respond to a persona which depended on them for its very existence.

Part of the quality of the myth sprang from its use of charm as a protective device. Coward was homosexual; this meant that, for most of his writing life, he was unable to give expression to what affected him most personally. If he was aware of the dangers of dealing directly onstage with gay sexuality – and the banning of his play *Semi-Monde*, which hints at homosexual relationships, would have left him in no doubt – he was also aware of the dangers of writing what was aesthetically false. His farewell play, *A Song at Twilight*, showed an ageing writer confronting the fact that he has sold out in his work by refusing to deal with his own sexuality. Coward's makeup in the role suggested Somerset Maugham, but it was also seen as poignantly autobiographical. Certainly some of Coward's love scenes are wooden in the extreme. But, in his major comedies, he achieved an eroticism that was strangely androgynous. Style and wit replace displays of physical passion because

Coward's dandaical characters cannot give themselves up to sex and retain their egoes; they are committed primarily not to people but to 'a gesture of defiance, a flower of vanity, courage and stupidity . . . the dandy's calculated insensibility, his grace and insolence.'[12] Gender becomes irrelevant. Laughter replaces lengthy displays of lovemaking, and the plays acquire greater energy and speed because of it. More important, perhaps, this androgyny plays merry hell with sexual stereotypes. In the best comedies only the dull characters are conventionally 'masculine' or 'feminine'. This subversion of social norms cuts across the political conservatism of Coward's work and contributes a sparkle and a welcome sense of danger.

Coward, of course, made capital out of both the subversion and the conservatism, out of work which pandered to his public and work which educated it. To understand him adequately it is essential to look at both aspects, to see his relationship with his public from all sides. What I hope to do in this book is, first, to look at Coward in the contexts that shaped him, charting the course of his work from the twenties to the sixties with a slightly different emphasis in each chapter. In looking at the Boy Wonder of the twenties I will examine the Edwardian skills that he brought to the new age and how he learned to use them to explore new *mores*. In dealing with the Coward of the thirties and the war years I shall be looking primarily at his instinct for satisfying public taste and public values. In the chapter concerned with his declining fortunes in the fifties and the period he called 'Dad's Renaissance' when he became a respected figure again, I shall be looking at the way in which he articulated, more or less for the first time, his ideas on the theatre. In the second part of the book I will deal separately with the enduring comedies and the kind of style they demand in the playing of them.

2
Society's Hero

I can remember. I can remember.
The months of November and December
Were filled for me with peculiar joys
So different from those of other boys
For other boys would be counting the days
Until the end of term and holiday times
But I was acting in Christmas plays
While they were taken to pantomimes.
I didn't envy their Eton suits,
Their children's dances and Christmas trees.
My life had wonderful substitutes
For such conventional treats as these.
I didn't envy their country larks,
Their organised games in panelled halls:
While they made snow-men in stately parks
I was counting the curtain calls.[1]

The image of the newly successful Noel Coward – one he
was not above fostering – is enshrined in a photograph in

17

the *Sketch* published during the run of *The Vortex*. He languishes in an elaborate bed wearing silk pyjamas, all the props required by any drawing-room comedy – telephone, cigarettes – at his side, over the caption 'Noel the Fortunate.' The reviews of *The Vortex* were guaranteed box office: 'A study of rottenness, of extravagant misery among extravagant pleasures' said *The Times*.[1a] For part of society at least the play *was* the twenties as they saw them. The second act curtain, in which the ageing actress explodes into hysteria as her lover leaves for a younger woman while her son plays a mounting jazz crescendo on the piano, was one of those moments that both shocked and satisfied the audience as Nora's slamming of the door in *The Doll's House* had done for a previous generation. It seemed a product of its time thrown up as naturally and as spontaneously as a champagne bubble, and Coward was confident enough of its reception to set a new theatrical precedent: the cast did not take the customary end-of-act curtain call but allowed the tension to remain unbroken till the end of the play, when, of course, the applause was tremendous.

This confidence reflected none of the backstage struggles. Coward's original leading lady had walked out: there were financial problems (his budget was £25 for the show) and his young designer Gladys Calthrop was forced to finish the set in the street: and there had been a last-minute battle with the censor in which Coward had to convince him that the play was really a moral tract. These struggles are closer to the truth about Coward's place in the twenties: he did not spring into them fully armed out of nothingness but from a solid background of professionalism which shaped his attitude to the times both offstage and on.

The sentimental little verse at the top of this chapter is

thus a more valuable clue to his way of working than the picture of the decadent *parvenu* in the dressing gown. Its nostalgia underlines the fact that Coward's roots lay in the Edwardian theatre of his childhood. Born a few weeks before the new century, he was working as an actor by the age of eleven. He learned from experience, not from study; while his autobiographies are reticent about personal relationships, they freely acknowledge his professional debts. He believed that experience was the only teacher; the advice his *alter ego* Garry Essendine gives to a would-be playwright is his own:

> If you wish to be a playwright you just leave the theatre of tomorrow to take care of itself. Go and get yourself a job as a butler in a repertory company if they'll have you. Learn from the ground up how plays are constructed and what is actable and what isn't. Then sit down and write at least twenty plays one after the other, and if you can manage to get the twenty-first produced for a Sunday night performance you'll be damned lucky!

Like the verse, this reflects a passion for the theatre, but there is a hidden corollary – a total acceptance of it, a lack of interest in experiment or change. Somewhere, Garry seems to be saying, there is a Platonic form called 'play' and your job is to get it right.

This was the attitude of the British theatre of Coward's day and continued to be so until the late fifties. European theatre was alive with change; Ibsen, Chekhov and Strindberg had already pushed back the frontiers of naturalism; by the time Coward came of age, Brecht, Wedekind, Pirandello and the Surrealists were changing the face of drama. The British reaction was hostility or unawareness; a 'play' meant a series of events which took place in a set with four walls; one wall was cut away to reveal people imitating real life, or at least selected aspects of it. Their net effect was to reinforce the *status quo*, in terms of class structures, religion, sexual relationships; individual characters might be seen to rebel, but the plays as a whole did not prompt questions. When rumblings of Continental discontent were voiced, they were generally censored or domesticated. Henry Arthur Jones, for example, rewrote *The Doll's House* and Nora, rechristened Flossie, came back through the famous door to her husband. After Shaw's Ibsenite play *Mrs. Warren's Profession* was banned (it only appeared in 1925, post-*Vortex*) he learned to sugar his social preoccupations with flippancy and created *Plays Pleasant*.

The most powerful forces in the theatre, in fact, were not writers or even critics, but the censors and the managements. Although hardly a year went by without a call for the abolition of the Lord Chamberlain's Office, Parliament invariably concluded that despite the odd mistake it was a Good Thing. Its views were slowly broadening as the new century advanced but it was always risky to submit a serious play on a potentially controversial theme; one might be told, as Beerbohm Tree was told in 1909 'that (the play) would be unacceptable . . . the subject was adultery – but if it could be made more comic, it would pass'.[2] Small wonder Henry James lamented that the British playwright's situation was the most undignified in Europe.

If the censor was one curb upon the playwright's potential, the financier was another. The National Theatre was a far-off dream. Occasionally groups like the Vedrenne–Barker management at the Court would make it possible for uncommercial writers to get a hearing. But on the whole plays which ignored the claims of the box office were doomed. Even Coward, astutely commercial as he was, had stormy passages in his nine-year association with one of the most powerful of all managers, C. B. Cochran, a man whose interests included not only Ibsen but flea circuses and plans for a pleasure park populated entirely by midgets.

These factors meant, inevitably, a limited range for the theatre. Formal experiment was almost impossible and no-one evolved a body of dramatic theory, like that of Brecht or Stanislavsky, in which to ground it. Theatrical debate confined itself to discussing what subjects and what kinds of language were permissible on the 'naturalistic' stage.

Coward's upbringing confirmed him in this mainstream tradition. His experience of it was fairly comprehensive. He appeared as a Mussel in Lila Field's *The Goldfish* (one of his rare appearances at the not-yet – Royal Court); as an angel in Hauptmann's expressionist play *Hannele*; as Slightly in *Peter Pan*; as a patriotic little boy in *War in the Air*, which announced itself in 1913 as 'designed to Arouse the National Consciousness to a Sense of its Hovering Peril'; as one of the Poppy Pierrots on the pier at Lee-on-Solent. He learned from all of these; even the patriotic spectacle re-surfaced in *Cavalcade* and the expressionist techniques in *Post Mortem*; the pierrots, and the Coward family passion for music taught him, as he put it, to 'take light music seriously'. He attended innumerable performances at the Gaiety Theatre, the birthplace of British musical comedy, where pieces like the *Quaker Girl* provided 'a happy combination between the continental operas of Offenbach and Lecoq, the comedy burlesques of the Old Gaiety Theatre and the healthy, clean-limbed but melodious high jinks of Gilbert and Sullivan'.[3] His own musical plays tried to catch their quality; he never trained as a musician but relied on what he called his 'perfect ear for pleasant sounds'.[4]

Most influential, however, were the plays in which he worked with Charles Hawtrey. He had one line in a Hawtrey play at the age of eleven and relentlessly dogged Hawtrey's footsteps at every subsequent engagement. Hawtrey's response was 'For God's sake leave me alone', but Coward continued to hang around and to draw conclusions about the art of comedy which he was never fundamentally to disown. Hawtrey was not a broad comic but a romantic comedian. He brought a new intimacy to the theatre after a period of Irvingesque declamation. His behaviour seemed casual, his lines thrown away – an apparent spontaneity which could only be achieved by superb breath control, great economy of action and underlying repose. He was frequently described as a gentleman, both offstage and on, a description which suggests both grace and restraint. His style depended heavily on personal magnetism. He was Wilde's original Lord Goring and his favourite role was always that of the attractive deceiver. 'When he fibbed he could not fail', recalled Ivor Brown.[5] His elegant deceptions gave him the detached air of a man 'watching himself go by', and meant too that for much of the play he was not himself delivering laugh lines but eliciting them from the other, deceived, characters. Coward seldom created this kind of role in his work but it was from this Hawtrey style that he drew his conviction that the secret of comedy lay in the placing and timing of the lines.

> . . . perfectly ordinary phrases such as 'just fancy!' should, by virtue of their context, achieve greater laughs than the most literate epigrams. Some of the biggest laughs in *Hay Fever* occur on such lines as 'Go on', 'No

there isn't, is there?' and 'This haddock's disgusting'. There are many other examples of my glittering sophistication in the same vein.[6]

Hawtrey's throwaway naturalism perhaps prompted him too to create dialogue that came a little closer to everyday speech than the stage had yet heard. Although Coward's name is hardly a by-word for naturalism now, in the twenties it seemed to Somerset Maugham that:

> It was inevitable that some dramatist should eventually write dialogue that exactly copied the average talk, with its hesitations, mumblings and repetitions, and broken sentences, of average people. I do not suppose that anyone can ever do this with more brilliant accuracy than Mr. Coward.[7]

If there was one major lesson to be learned from the pre-war British Theatre, however, it was that of construction. The term 'well-made play' has acquired slightly pejorative connotations over the years, but it accurately sums up the attitude to playmaking prevalent throughout most of Coward's lifetime. It originated with the work of Scribe in France but became chiefly associated with the work of Pinero and Maugham, and with the virtues extolled in William Archer's book *Playmaking*. Its subtitle, 'A Manual of Craftsmanship', reflects the audience's main expectation. Craftsmanship is a skill; it is essential to create a work that is solid as well as attractive, a Hepplewhite chair, for instance. But craftsmanship does not necessarily mean innovation, and the audience for a 'well-made' play expected it to have a familiar shape. A story would be developed across the first act, reach an exciting climax at the end of the second and find a resolution in the third.

There were shocks and surprises, but generally of the same kind – rooted in the characters, in particular in their past lives; writers gained much dramatic mileage out of compromising letters or former lovers turning up unexpectedly, and they expected a very specific response to these revelations. The myth of 'craftsmanship' is that it is 'unobtrusive', that clues must be planted with great subtlety and the surprises carefully plotted. In fact, the well-made play is a code to which the audience holds the key. They join with the dramatist to pretend that life is artfully shaped, that we do indeed make helpfully expository remarks to our friends and servants. (Towards the end of the well-made play's run of popularity it was also necessary to pretend that most people *had* servants, but they made such convenient expository tools that most audiences did.) They agree to pretend that life is shaped in a series of key scenes; *scène à faire* was a favourite term of Scribe's and most English plays in the convention have one scene on which all the audience's hope of good entertainment is fixed. Marriages are made or broken in single incidents, not in complex processes; confrontations are prepared for and then issues decided at once. In the classic British example of the genre, *The Second Mrs. Tanqueray*, the eponymous heroine, a woman with a past, discovers that her sweet young step-daughter is about to marry her former lover Ardale. Clearly the play centres on the inevitable scene between Mrs Tanqueray and Ardale, and when it happens everything is cut and dried. They agree to Tell All, the marriage is forbidden and Mrs Tanqueray commits repentant suicide. Nowhere is there a hint of the messy business that this kind of relationship might really entail, the conflicting emotions and moral pressures that would change from day to day. Not, one presumes, because Pinero was unaware of them but because they do not fit the form, because they would force the audience to think about relationships in general and not about the skill with which the plot is made.

Coward admired these plays and in *Present Indicative* paid tribute to Gilbert Miller, the producer who first reinforced this lesson in relation to his own work. Coward sent him his first play, a melodrama called *The Last Trick*; Miller's advice was that the 'construction of a play was as important as the foundations of a house, whereas dialogue, however good, could only, at best, be considered as interior decoration'.[8] This concern for construction was to serve him well in the lightest and best comedies, providing a backbone to the frivolity and giving it the conviction of a carefully thought-out attitude. When, however, he had something more serious to say the form could prove constricting, as we shall see. Coward recognised that the Edwardian well-made play was a true mirror of its times in its limitations as well as its strengths:

All of these 'drawing-room dramas' dealt with the psychological and social problems of the upper middle classes. The characters in them were, as a general rule, wealthy, well-bred, articulate and motivated by the exigencies of the world to which they belonged. This world was snobbish, conventional, polite, and limited by its own codes and rules of behaviour, and it was the contravention of these codes and rules – to our eyes so foolish and old-fashioned – that supplied the dramatic content . . . it is easy nowadays to laugh at these vanished moral attitudes, but they were poignant enough in their own time because they were true.[9]

His relationship with the form was complex; he saw himself to some extent as impacting the well-made play on his own times rather than as creating something new. Sometimes the old skins exploded under the pressure of the new wine; sometimes they held; sometimes the result was an interesting new shape. Before looking at the plays in which Coward the writer learned his craft in the twenties, however, it is necessary to look at the new audience for which he was writing them.

The twenties were the period in which England began painfully to come to terms with the impact of the First World War. Wilfred Owen had written in the preface to his poems that 'This book is not about heroes. English poetry is not yet fit to speak of them,'[10] but it seemed that for the first ten years or so of the aftermath England as a whole was not willing to speak of them. Those who had remained at home remained ignorant of what their returning soldiers had been through and only in the latter half of the decade did they begin to publish their own experiences, in what Alan Jenkins called 'books . . . which had red labels from the library . . . and were hidden under cushions'.[11] It was said that half the chorus boys in the Hippodrome revues had the MC or the DSO, reflecting the economic conditions which failed to supply the 'Homes for heroes' and the desire to forget the past. Suggestions that the existing economic system was breaking down were countered by pointing out the flourishing state of companies like Ford's in the USA and by platitudes about the inevitable but temporary consequences of war. The majority of people were extremely conservative in outlook. There was widespread fear of the more radical kind of socialism, to the extent that the Labour government of 1924 could be brought down by a forged letter alleging a plot with 'Moscow'.

But if it took the General Strike and the spectacle of the Wall Street Crash across the water to bring home the vast contrast between rich and poor, to dramatise class divisions in a way that could not be ignored, another kind of social division was very apparent – that between old and young. 'Old Man' became the worst insult that the younger generation could apply to the old, the vengeful old Abraham who had killed not only his son but 'half the seed of Europe, one by one',[12] the men who had been responsible for the war but sent another generation to fight it. Both the survivors of the war and, even more, the younger people who had grown up in their shadow, were affected by the cult of Youth. One obvious manifestation of it was the phenomenon of the Bright Young Things. The term was coined by the *Daily Mail*; like most mass-media terms ('mods and rockers', for example) it was an amalgam of truth and fiction, a simplified version of reality but not wholly false. The Bright Young Things were a tiny minority of the population, a group of upper-class young people who conducted a very public social life; they held enormously expensive parties with themes: people came dressed as babies, or in eighteenth-century clothes; they conducted treasure hunts, including one which reduced Selfridge's to chaos; they devised elaborate practical jokes. On the whole they were famous for being famous rather than for any special activity, although some dabbled in the arts. (Coward was to object violently to the presence of 'society ladies' among the extras in *Cavalcade*.) They gave the press a good time deploring their antics to the point of tedium; as Waugh put it in *Vile Bodies*, 'the topic of the Younger Generation spread through the company like a yawn'.[13] Some flirted with fascism but their net effect on politics was to shore up the *status quo*; they redeemed themselves in the eyes of the mainly right-wing popular press by their conduct during the General Strike, which afforded them yet another opportunity to dress up. As the *Illustrated*

London News put it, 'We feel that the heart of England must be sound . . . when we read that Mr. C. E. Pitman, the Oxford Stroke, is driving a train . . . Lord Chesham is driving a train and the Hon. Lionel Tennyson is a Special.'[14]

But if their politics were conservative they nonetheless symbolised a social change. Their clothes and attitudes did not just demonstrate wealth but provided an outward symbol of a new kind of sexual behaviour. They embraced the looser, more revealing and more comfortable clothes of Chanel and Molyneux, clothes which were strongly influenced by sportswear and allowed ease of movement. They demonstrated that women had new spheres of activity outside the home and were not expected to wait in corseted obedience for a husband to come along. New names were bandied about. Most people had at least a hazy notion of Freud's work on sexuality and the unconscious. Contraception was available and Marie Stopes inserted discreet advertisements in the Press.

The fact that society chose the Bright Young Things to symbolise these changes suggests, perhaps, that it was having trouble thinking them through. It is interesting that, in the literature of the period, much of the most creative work was being done by people who considered themselves apart from society – people who were not English, like Eliot, Pound, Conrad, Yeats; people of working-class origin, like Lawrence; or people who created their own self-enclosed world like the Bloomsbury set. While they were changing the shape of literature, indigenous writers adopted a tone which hovered between cynicism and a kind of futile anger. Waugh, for instance, showed the twenties young as greedy, joylessly promiscuous and racked by scandal, although he described himself as one of the Bright Young Things too. Huxley showed them as callously indifferent to poverty and deprivation but never managed to suggest alternatives. Meanwhile, popular literature reflected a blandly enjoyable vision of the *status quo* – the golden age of the detective story had begun – or exploited the new sexual *mores* while retaining a foot in Victorian values.

Two novels aptly symbolise the period and sum up the tastes to which Coward's early work was to appeal; interestingly enough they both had a substantial effect on his finances. Margaret Kennedy's *The Constant Nymph* brought him success in the part of Lewis Dodd when the book was dramatised. Michael Arlen made his fortune with *The Green Hat* and came to the financial rescue of *The Vortex*. Both books deal with aspects of sexuality which hover on the fringes of convention and both use death as a convenient escape clause. *The Constant Nymph* deals with the relationship between a composer and a waif from a large Bohemian family. They run away together, seeking to avoid the spiritual shackles of conventional marriage, but the girl, who is only fifteen, thoughtfully dies before they can consummate their love or obligate the author to confront the issues that it raises. *The Green Hat* is even better at having its moral cake and eating it. The heroine, described as having 'bad blood', leads a promiscuous life and, unable to marry her true love, takes on a war hero who jumps out of the window on their wedding night. She allows the world to believe that he was prompted by her infidelity. It is only before her own spectacular suicide, driving her Hispano into a tree she has named 'Harrods' that she reveals that he was overcome with guilt because he had syphilis. In both works potentially serious contemporary issues are raised and then avoided with slick sensationalism.

The plays of Coward's apprenticeship explore the new

mores more cautiously and more thoughtfully. The first performable play he wrote, *The Rat Trap*, looked at a modern marriage and the attempt of a young couple to ground it in true equality. Sheila and Keld are writers. Coward makes it apparent that Sheila has real talent, while Keld has a developing gift for writing commercial drama. Increasingly after the honeymoon Sheila compromises and suppresses her genius in order to keep the marriage together, while Keld forges ahead with his successful pot-boilers. At the second act curtain Sheila's frustration finally explodes:

> Olive warned me and it's come true: we're like two rats in a trap, fighting, fighting, fighting. You need a commonplace, dull, domesticated wife with no brain and boundless open-mouthed appreciation for every mortal thing you do – someone who would hang on your words and convince you all the time of your own incredible brilliance; the sort of woman who would be tactful when you were fractious and upset, and affectionate when you felt in the mood for it, which would be in the evening over a well-cooked and well-ordered dinner, and you'd stroke her hair and dole out a few well-chosen words of praise – not too many for fear of making her conceited – and there would never be a single moment in the day or night when you wouldn't be absolutely, unconditionally satisfied with yourself. With a larger mind you'd be a brute – but you're too contemptible even for that.

Keld promptly hits her and she walks out. In the third act she learns that she is pregnant and goes glumly back to him. Coward later described this ending as sentimental. In this he was unfair to himself: the pregnancy is not surrounded by the conventional rosy glow. It does, however, give a false air of finality to the play: the issues he has raised are too complex to fit the 'well-made' convention. And while passages like Sheila's tirade express the truth of the situation, they are verbose and flabby, spelling out painfully what we have already seen. The play was, however, a flag planted by the eighteen-year-old Coward in the territory of youth and talent.

His next two plays had fun with similar themes. *I'll Leave it to You*, his first play to be performed (1920) shows they young Dermotts, bereaved and broke, galvanised into activity by the promise of a legacy from their Uncle Daniel, to go to whichever of them makes good in his last remaining years of life. Inevitably all succeed, transformed from dilettantes into a film star, a painter, a writer, a composer and an engineer; and, just as inevitably, Uncle Daniel proves to be in the best of health and completely penniless. It is a predictable plot and Coward makes intelligent use of it; we see through Uncle Daniel at once and are free to enjoy his charm and resourcefulness; he launches into elaborate descriptions of his life in the wilds of South America, demanding full audience participation and making capital out of his innumerable slips in geography; at the end of the play a telegram arrives to say that gold has been found in his useless mine. As the curtain falls his favourite niece asks 'Did you send that telegram to yourself?' and he replies with an unrepentant 'Yes.'

The Young Idea was staged in 1922 and marked a step forward. Again the tone was frivolous and the subject was youth and charm, but this time the charm had a real purpose. Sholto and Gerda, twins who owe a good deal to Philip and Dolly in Shaw's *You Never Can Tell*, decide to re-unite their estranged parents. Talented performers, they have a range of techniques at their disposal but the object of their charm is always the same – to expose dull and false feelings and stir up the remembrance of love. The family comes together at the end because they can see through themselves and everyone else; to Coward this was an essential attribute of charm and a touchstone of worth. Thus Sholto and Gerda make their first entrance in the style of Victorian sentimental drama. 'Are you our daddy?', they sob brokenly to George, and collapse in delight when he plays up to them with 'Little girl – sonny – may I call you sonny . . .'

James Agate praised the play for the way in which the wit was integrated into the dialogue:

> Mr. Coward is not only witty, but is also clever at covering up his wit. 'I did not drive you into your lover's arms,' says Brent. 'Why should I? You were trotting there quite comfortably of your own accord.' 'You use banter to conceal your lack of courage,' retorts Cicely. Now, this is very neat cover. Brent's remark, we had felt, did not proceed out of the situation, but purely out of the author's inability to resist a, for the once, rather poor joke. Banter being conceded, our objections fade away and we are floated over to the next consideration, that of George's courage.[15]

The integration, however, goes deeper than this; banter *is* courage, or at least moral strength. Sholto and Gerda expose the dull duplicity of the 'county' set with whom their father has got embroiled by his new wife Cicely, through an assumed and lethal innocence; they toy artlessly with horsey expressions like 'a good seat' and enquire naively why getting drunk at a hunt ball is a 'damn good rag'. They draw George into their double act with a spell-binding account of an imaginary reunion between husband and wife, leaving out not a single detail:

GERDA: The Orient Express! We get into it about
    seven-thirty and have dinner as we whizz through the
    suburbs –
SHOLTO: Then we come back and find our wagons-lits have
    been made up so we sit in rather strained positions and
    play games –
GERDA: Clumps, and Being People in History!

With both parents, they share their charm rather than use it
to deceive. Lies only work on dull people: to a gossipy
friend of Cicely they offer a story about their drunken
mother: to an unwanted suitor of their mother a story about
a husband in an asylum. The symmetry is typical of
Coward's developing skill in construction; its artifice
reinforces the atmosphere of play.

Coward also tried to handle the longing for charm.
Sirocco told the story of a young Englishwoman who leaves
her dull husband for a half-Italian painter, Sirio. When her
husband discovers them in the squalor of Sirio's flat, she
sends him away, saying that they have never loved each
other; then she turns on Sirio too for reducing her dreams
to a sordid and cheap reality. As the curtain falls she cries
'I'm free – free for the first time in my life. God help me.'
leaving us with a situation more potentially interesting than
the play. The problem with *Sirocco* is that although it
creates effectively the silliness of the girl and the second-
rate charm of Sirio, it fails to convey the erotic glamour
they originally see in each other. It was a brave attempt, for
its time, to explore the gap between sexual passion and the
aura of magic that surrounds it; it was brave, too, when the
play finally came to be performed, to cast Ivor Novello as
Sirio. Novello, usually cast as romantic hero, exploited to
the full the contrast between his Valentino beauty and the
dinginess of Sirio's inner life. Ultimately the play is earnest

but dull, although it was clearly a worthwhile exercise in preparation for *The Vortex*.

Coward meanwhile kept himself vigorously in the public eye. He played leading parts in his own plays; he visited America, and though he failed to find work there he learned a respect for the pace and speed of American acting and an understanding of the new jazz rhythms that were beginning to creep across the Atlantic. Both of these he adapted for his own purposes. He grafted the jazz beat onto his own romantically pretty, English style of songwriting and created complex effects. In the Charlot revue *London Calling!* he provided an image for the times in the song *Parisian Pierrot*: it was attractively lyrical but mixed with the acid of the blues; Gertrude Lawrence sang it to the figure of a Pierrot doll with a kind of weary tenderness that made it the most lasting number in the show.

All in all, he had given himself a solid apprenticeship and was now on the verge of writing the plays that made his name in the twenties – *Fallen Angels*, *The Vortex*, *Hay Fever*, *Easy Virtue* and his revue *On With the Dance*, all composed (along with some less successful pieces) between 1923 and 1925. The fact that *The Vortex* was the first to be staged illustrates Coward's instinct as a total man of the theatre rather than a playwright. Norman MacDermott of the Everyman Theatre in Hampstead agreed to present *Hay Fever* or *The Vortex*: Coward astutely talked him into selecting the latter because it contained, as he put it, 'a whacking good part for myself'.[16] The part was not simply 'good'; it also landed Coward squarely in the midst of a controversy about theatre and permitted him to become symbol and spokesman for a new generation. In response to the inevitable wrath of outraged Edwardians (Sir Gerald du Maurier described the play as 'the younger generation knocking on the door of the dustbin'), Coward called for reforms. He suggested 'a few clear-thinking young men and women' should join the Board of Censors and demanded new standards of writing:

> When the self-advertising denouncers of the stage describe the English theatre as being in a 'disgraceful state' they speak a bitter truth without being aware of it. It is in a disgraceful state, but for none of the reasons so far put forward. The actual cause of the very definite decline of our drama is that at least ninety per cent of the people at present concerned in it are mentally incapable of regarding it as art at all.[17]

The Vortex is an intriguing mixture. On the one hand it has firm roots in the nineteenth century. It has affinities with the Shavian/Ibsenite 'problem play'. Nicky's cocaine, Florence's lovers, are the equivalent of the inherited syphilis of *Ghosts* or Mrs Warren's unmentionable profession. The structure is close to the well-made drawing-room plays of Pinero. It opens with a standard expository device: friends of the main characters discuss them in their absence and establish the play's *milieu*. Coward then goes on to outline the main relationships: we meet Florence and her young lover, Tom, already a little embarrassed by her; we see her dull-but-decent husband and their son Nicky, who has just returned from Paris. We meet Nicky's fiancée, Bunty, and the curtain falls on a Pinero-like revelation that Tom and Bunty 'used to know one another awfully well'.

The second act finds all the characters in Florence's country house and here Coward springs a series of surprises, again in the Pinero tradition. Tom becomes ill at ease with Florence; Nicky quarrels with Bunty. Inevitably, Tom and Bunty fall into each other's arms. But Coward adds an extra twist: Nicky has a heart-to-heart with Florence's kind friend Helen and reveals his dependence on cocaine. The 'strong curtain' at the end of the act pulls all the threads together; Florence discovers Tom and Bunty; Nicky responds not only with the anger of the abandoned lover but with that of the betrayed son and with the hysteria generated by cocaine. The third act contains the *scène à faire* to which we have been looking forward in the interval: the confrontation between Nicky and his mother. In fact this takes up the whole act; the curtain falls on Florence mechanically stroking her son's hair and contemplating his stricken future in a tableau reminiscent of the end of *Ghosts*.

Photographs of the original production reinforce this impression of a nineteenth-century play. Lilian Braithwaite as Florence throws herself an Nicky's feet with an abandon suggestive of a Fallen Woman in Victorian melodrama; Coward as Nicky smites his forehead in a gesture that looks strangely at odds with the modish dressing-gown of the period. But if the form and the gestures were old, the subject matter and style were so new as to be shocking. Drugs had never been mentioned on stage. The nervy, suppressed hysteria with which Coward invested Nicky made him an exciting if not admirable character. And the play had a new kind of energy. The old well-made play had had countless twists and turns of plot, and imparted quantities of information. Coward jettisoned most of this in favour of atmosphere. The second act, for instance, opened with a scene so stylised as to be almost expressionistic:

EVERYONE MUST APPEAR TO BE SPEAKING AT ONCE, BUT THE ACTUAL LINES SPOKEN WHILE DANCING MUST BE TIMED TO REACH THE AUDIENCE AS THE SPEAKERS PASS NEAR THE

*FOOTLIGHTS. THIS SCENE WILL PROBABLY BE
EXCEEDINGLY DIFFICULT TO PRODUCE, BUT
IT IS ABSOLUTELY INDISPENSIBLE.*

HELEN: It's much too fast, Nicky.

TOM: Do slow down a bit.

NICKY: It's the pace that's marked on the record.

PAWNIE: I've never danced well since the War, I don't
know why.

FLORENCE: But your last act was so strong, when she came
in half mad with fright and described everything
minutely.

BRUCE: I try to write as honestly as possible.

CLARA: I gave her three for manners, but seven for
charm, because I had to be a little nice!

TOM: I thought she was a rather decent sort.

BUNTY: No, but really Nicky, his technique completely
annihilated his inspiration.

The virtual isolation of each speech reflects the selfishness
and the spiritual desolation of Florence and Nicky's world,
and conveys it with a speed that a conventional exposition
could not. Similarly the endless jazz music, heard
throughout, acts almost as another character. It says what
the others cannot, and for Nicky the piano provides a
mouthpiece for his feelings about Bunty and Florence.
Boldly, Coward then set the last act against the contrast
of utter silence.

But *The Vortex* did more than make a few technical
innovations. It crystallised ideas only partly expressed in
Coward's early plays: here, for the first time, Coward
provided the youth of his generation with a style and a
self-image: many of them who had never seen the play still

responded to it as disseminated through the press and through his music. *The Vortex*, first of all, stressed the centrality of the young in the new world. Reading early Coward after reading, say, a piece by Pinero or Maugham, always gives one a mental picture of much younger actors. In the old well-made plays the young were there as images of innocence, to provide a sub-plot or a little lyrical relief; in Coward's plays of the twenties the young are the people who make the plot happen, the moving spirits of the action. They are physically vigorous; *The Vortex* contains a great deal of dancing. They are edgy and nervous – the fashionable complaint of the time was 'neurasthenia' – but Coward the actor, playing Nicky, made this physically attractive and exciting; Sybil Thorndike recalls him as a great 'hysterical' actor, charged with energy. 'You see,' she recalled, 'he could SCREAM!'.[18] Coward elevated the fashionable slang, with its gushing epithets like 'divine' and its casual endearments like 'darling' into a language; it expressed not just a new and more permissive attitude to relationships but a clear-sighted cynicism about the world. In one of the most popular plays of a previous generation, Maugham's *Lady Frederick*, the heroine's central gesture had caused a sensation: she had shown herself to her naive young admirer without make-up and destroyed his illusions for his own good. But in *The Vortex* it is Nicky who sweeps away the contents of his mother's dressing-table; it is the young who stand for the truth. The popular hard-boiled pose of the twenties here acquired a metaphysic. Coward added a melancholy grace note by stressing the transience of youth:

NICKY: You're frightfully hard, Bunty.
BUNTY: Am I?
NICKY: Much harder than me – really.

BUNTY: You've got so much hysteria.

NICKY: I can't help it.

BUNTY: Of course not – it's your temperament. You burst out suddenly.

NICKY: Not so badly as I used to.

BUNTY: You're growing older.

NICKY: God, yes; isn't it foul?

BUNTY: Hell, my dear.

NICKY: It's funny how mother's generation always longed to be old when they were young, and we strain every nerve to keep young.

BUNTY: That's because we see what's coming so much more clearly.

He also offered a welcome reassurance that moral standards were not so different after all, that the young were not completely adrift from the past. At the end of *The Vortex* Nicky throws his box of cocaine out of the window. One sympathises with the stagehand who, new to the play, kindly threw it back in case he needed it; as an estimate of Nicky's character it was probably just. But Coward's instinct was for the strong curtain and the thumpingly moral conclusion.

This typified his role in the twenties. He provided an imitable physical style: his polo sweaters became a fashionable craze, his clipped voice was widely copied. He gave the young a pose to strike, cynical, pleasure-seeking, witty and tough. But he also provided them, in his own person, with a sort of moral Dutch uncle. In *Poor Little Rich Girl* he sang:

> The role you are acting
> The toll is exacting,
> Soon you'll have to pay.

The music of living
You lose in the giving,
False things soon decay.
These words from me may surprise you,
I've no right to advise you,
I've known life too well, dear,
Your own life must tell, dear,
Please don't turn away.

He was ostensibly addressing the wealthy section of society, but in a way that shrewdly popularised his message; life, he pointed out, is not all it's cracked up to be for the rich, and one could participate in their worldly-wise disillusion for the price of a record or some sheet music even if theatre tickets were too expensive. By the disarming 'I've no right to advise you', Coward implied that he had plumbed the depths and come back safe to guide others through the tangles of sophistication.

The solidly conservative moral base of his work was not apparent to everyone; although St. John Irvine remarked 'I protest against the assumption, now too commonly made, that Mr Coward is a flippant youth who delights in the pretence that vice is virtue',[19] others abused him for pandering to a current taste for 'sex plays' (Sir Gerald du Maurier's phrase). *Fallen Angels*, for instance, drew considerable flak, although in retrospect this cheerful trifle about two young married women getting drunk as they await the visit of a mutual ex-lover seems harmlessly comic rather than an invitation to debauchery.

By June 1925, *The Vortex*, *Hay Fever*, *Fallen Angels* and *On With the Dance* were all running in the West End. A year later, the King and Queen attended the London opening of *Easy Virtue*. It was a significant choice of play; George V and Queen Mary epitomised the family-centred virtues that the previous King had somewhat undermined and by attending a work which Coward described as 'similar in form and tone and plot to the plays of Pinero'[20] they were affording him the accolade of respectability, an acknowledgement that he spoke for a wider audience than would-be Bright Young Things.

Easy Virtue is an interesting rather than a successful play, precisely because of its adherence to the well-made form. Its subject is the Woman with a Past familiar to Edwardian audiences; the *New York Times* called it '*The Second Mrs. Tanqueray* brought down to date.'[21] When John Whittaker brings his once-divorced wife Larita back to his country home it is clear that the reaction of the society she encounters there will be the centre of the play, just as Edwardian society's reaction to Paula Tanqueray was the *raison-d'être* of the older play. But life, and society's options, had changed. When Aubrey Tanqueray marries Paula, they both expect, correctly, two possible responses: Christian forgiveness or the rough justice of ostracism. When Paula dies her pious stepdaughter wishes, not that she had been less priggish or more accepting of a lifestyle different from her own, but that she had shown 'mercy'. It is clear from the moment Larita walks in and treats her new relations with friendly self-possession that she is not interested in 'mercy,' although their attitude to her resembles young Miss Tanqueray's to Paula.

Pinero, though, could take these attitudes for granted in his own world. They were instinctive, backed up by a system of beliefs which his audience largely shared. Coward, however, had to find a motivation for them. He did so, in the very un-Pinero-like form of sexual repression. He describes the unpleasant Mrs Whittaker in a rather malicious stage direction as:

the type of woman who has the reputation of having been 'quite lovely' as a girl. The stern repression of any sex emotions all her life has brought her to middle age with a faulty digestion which doesn't so much sour her temper as spread it. She views the world with the jaundiced eyes of a woman who subconsciously realises she has missed something, which means in point of fact that she has missed everything.

He plays an enjoyable series of variations on this theme. John's repression manifests itself in moral cowardice, his sister Marion's in an excessively hearty and hygienic frankness. Given this unattractive motivation behind their rejection of Larita, it is clear that she will become not their outcast but their judge. They gossip about her, rake up episodes from her past and present them in the worst possible light, and wilfully misinterpret the dawning friendship between her and Colonel Whittaker, until she finally explodes with a judgement which echoes Coward's own. 'All your life,' she announces, 'you've ground down perfectly natural sex impulses until your mind has become a morass of inhibitions.' Mrs Whittaker promptly orders her to her room and withdraws the invitation to attend a party that night. As the curtain falls on the second act we see Larita smashing a plaster statuette of the Venus de Milo and collapsing with shaking shoulders, but 'whether from laughter or tears it is difficult to say.'

This moment symbolises the contradictions which tend to pull the play apart. It is never certain whether Coward simply wants us to laugh at the Whittakers or to see them as a real threat to Larita's happiness. It is hard to imagine that she could even want to be accepted by them. Coward also seems to shift the ground of the conflict in an uneasy way, loading the dice against the Whittakers on more than one level. At times he portrays with conviction the conflict between repression and honesty; one of Lari's finest gestures at the party she defiantly attends in the third act is to greet a local woman who has thrown out her maid because Mrs Whittaker disapproves of her with the trenchant remark 'I'm sure she'll get on in the profession you've sent her to.' He celebrates the moral courage of charm; at the awkward first meeting between Larita and the Whittakers, she displays tact and grace with 'How do you do seems so hopelessly inadequate, doesn't it, at a moment like this? But perhaps it's good to use it as a refuge for our real feelings.' She meets in return a chilly display of Mrs Whittaker's 'real' feelings, already formulated despite the fact that she has never seen Larita before. Her exit too is managed with grace; she gently teaches John the bitter truth that their passion has died, tactfully and without rancour.

But while we are rightly asked to applaud Larita's integrity and good manners, and her honesty in following her sexual nature, Coward also seems to expect us to treat the most superficial aspects of charm with the same wholehearted reverence. He complained that when his original leading lady, Jane Cowl, smashed the statuette, she made it a tragic moment when he wanted a comic climax to the act; in a way, however, he was forcing the 'tragic' conclusion upon us. We are expected to see Larita as more 'cultured' than her in-laws: as evidence of this she is seen reading Proust indoors rather than playing tennis; she asks for champagne at the party and for 'plain water' if there is none; one of her first questions to Mrs Whittaker is 'does your butler speak French?'. At times, indeed, it seems as if Coward is identifying charm with money rather than as a real social or personal grace. The play can look alarmingly like a snob's guide: Paris is good, the English

43

countryside bad: the Ritz is good, plaster statues are bad: Cartier cigarette cases are morally impeccable, evening dresses with matching handbags morally suspect.

This springs from the fact that Coward had to strain for his effects. Lari, in 1924, was not threatened by the social code of the day as Paula was and did not have to make the stark choice of conformity or social expulsion. When she goes off to the Ritz, where she 'always' goes to mend her broken heart, we sense that she will soon pick up the pieces. Coward had to introduce secondary themes, like that of taste, to reinforce the play. It is, in a sense, as John Russell Taylor described it, 'an attempt to write a well-made drama about the impossibility of writing well-made dramas any more'[22] and represents, perhaps, Coward's desire to expand his audience rather than his fully-thought-out conclusions about the form or the matter.

The next few years marked the end of the honeymoon between Coward and his public. He had some success with his Ruritanian fantasy *The Queen was in the Parlour*, and with the frilly eighteenth-century comedy *The Marquise*. On the whole, however, the later twenties were marked by problems with public and censor. He wrote a couple of new comedies, *This Was a Man* and *Home Chat*. The former was banned in England because the Lord Chamberlain's Office objected to the moment when the hero, learning of his wife's infidelity, burst out laughing; in America it was considered 'trifling'. The latter drew from the gallery on the first night the shouted comment 'We expected better.' Both plays, as Coward himself later admitted, were 'dead failures' and the audience were right to object to them as sub-standard. The traumatic first night of *Sirocco* in 1927 throws a more interesting light on Coward's relationship with his audience; here their reaction seemed to spring less from the conviction that the play was not a good one

(Coward's own verdict of 'a little better than bad but not quite good enough' is fair) than from resentment at the subject matter. His treatment of the feeble heroine and the seedy, callous hero seemed to deny the existence of 'romance'; by casting Ivor Novello as a phoney and vicious Don Juan he offended the sensibilities of many theatre-goers who had fancied themselves worldly-wise when they were watching *The Vortex*. There were, it seemed, certain areas which the public would still not allow to be explored.

Coward's more adventurous side was also checked by the outright banning of his play *Semi-Monde*. Written in 1926, it had to wait for production until 1977. The reason, presumably, was that the Lord Chamberlain's Office objected to the fact that Coward showed some relationships which were evidently homosexual; in an era when the prevalent attitude to homosexuality was neatly summed up by George V ('thought fellows like that shot themselves') the ban was inevitable. By 1977 the more likely objections were that Coward tended to fall into camp stereotypes and that the transition of one of the more attractive characters from gay to 'straight' relationships had offensive implications. For its time, however, the play was a bold experiment, not just in subject but in form. Set in the public rooms of the Paris Ritz, it consists entirely of scenes that, in most plays, would form the opening exposition or transition passages before a major scene. The forty characters order drinks, exchange greetings, pause to chat, glance at one another and walk on, ask casually after mutual acquaintances. It seems completely without plot or structure. Only one real 'incident' occurs, when one man shoots his rival in love; characteristically, it is placed well into the third act, almost by the way. But in fact *Semi-Monde* is very precisely crafted and controlled. Through the apparently aimless chat he charts a number of stories in detail; we see love affairs blossom and die; a young woman grows from naive teenager to gold-digger; a group of women form complex alliances and intrigues over their various lovers; a young couple, Owen and Tanis, plan to be 'awfully true' to one another: they meet a novelist and his daughter and their relationship becomes painful and complicated.

The Glasgow Citizen's production of the play in 1977 expanded the three-year time scheme; a bellboy wandered through each act, paging 'Mrs Wallis Warfield', then 'Mrs Wallis Simpson' and finally 'Her Grace'; the Ritz world gradually took on a darker tone and the reminder that we were, with the Abdication and its aftermath, only three years away from war, seemed timely and true to the spirit of the play. It seemed like an elegy for the pre-war years. If Coward had continued to develop on the lines of *Semi-Monde* his work might have taken a very different turn; as it is, it remains an enigma rich in unfulfilled possibilities.

When he did bounce back into public favour, however, he was indeed already beginning to look back on the twenties. His revue *This Year of Grace* played to packed houses and critical acclaim; Virginia Woolf admired it and St. John Irvine's *Observer* review consisted of an alphabetical list of superlatives. There was an ingratiating parody of the *Sirocco* disaster and a last sad song for the poor little rich girl, *Dance Little Lady*. The staging was more dramatic than that of the *On with the Dance* number: here Lauri Devine danced frenziedly, pursued by masked figures; the accent was less on moral danger than the inevitable prospect of burnout and exhaustion.

> Nigger melodies
> Syncopate your nerves
> Till your body curves

Drooping – stooping.
Laughter someday dies
And when the lights are starting to gutter
Dawn through the shutter
Shows you're living in a world of lies.

The same melancholy underlay *Private Lives*, the Coward play which ushered in the thirties. And in his last work to be produced in the twenties, Coward showed that he had already anticipated and adapted to changes in public taste. *Bitter-Sweet*, therefore, will be treated in the next chapter.

3
Consider the Audience . . .

The actor-playwright Emlyn Williams likes to tell the story of his big break that never happened in 1929. 'Just before Christmas I lost, in mid-rehearsal, a wonderful small part in *Tunnel Trench* at the Duchess. ("A little too emotional" – too *emotional*, the boy was dying in a shell-hole!)'[1] The story in many ways symbolises the theatrical, and indeed social climate that was to prevail throughout the thirties and into the war years. 'Youth' was no longer a magical word. Although the new attitudes to sex and marriage were to remain, the sense of hectic glamour they had brought in their wake had faded. The *angst* of the twenties and its attempts to shut out the memories of war underlay the decade's most fashionable ailment, neurasthenia. 'Nerves' drove Nicky and the Poor Little Rich Girl, and indeed Coward himself. The diagnosis of the thirties was more sombre – 'anxiety', the sense of ill-being summed up at the close of *Cavalcade* in *Twentieth Century Blues*:

Consider the Audience . . .

> What is there to strive for,
> Love, or keep alive for? Say –
> Hey, hey, call it a day.
> Blues,
> Nothing to win or lose.
> It's getting me down.

Anxiety operated on many levels. The post-war slump did not end. One third of the population lived for the whole decade beneath the poverty line; another third only just reached it. Britain went off the gold standard and the Labour Government collapsed. The General Election of October 1931 brought in the National Government whose approach to its massive problems was 'safety first'. It brought in the means test and made life even less tolerable for a large section of the population. The decade was marked by hunger marches and by a singular combination of caution and despair. Desparate solutions were glimpsed at: at one point the *Sunday Dispatch* offered prizes for the best essay on 'Why I like the Blackshirts'. There was still a widespread fear of 'socialism'; it seemed safer to put one's trust in 'commonsense' political slogans like Baldwin's dreary dictum 'first-rate minds have second-rate characters.'

At the same time there was a widespread and growing conviction that another war was inevitable. Coward himself articulated it in his war play *Post Mortem*, written in 1930. While some the the best-known books and plays of the First World War were finally making their appearance – *Goodbye to All That*, *All Quiet in the Western Front*, *Journey's End*, *The Silver Tassie* – there was an accompanying awareness that the next war would be very different; the war literature enshrined a lost generation sunk in its own myth rather than commenting on the new times.

It was a period rich in political writing, some of it factual, documentary, some of it, such as the poetry of Auden, Spender, and Day-Lewis, attempting to understand the relationship between the private self and the public one, to get to grips not only with a political vision but with the literary impact of Modernism; there was a new awareness of Europe and of events beyond our own borders. Novels such as *Stamboul Train* and *Goodbye to Berlin* reflected a typical preoccupation with the image of crossing borders and frontiers. Even writers concerned with the realistic depiction of the lower middle-class *milieu* seem inbued with a sense of frustration at their own tight limits. Wells's Mr Polly and Orwell's George Bowling, for instance, both indulge in a kind of pastoral dream of a society somehow freer and pleasanter than their own. Theirs is, as Terry Eagleton puts it, 'a world intelligent enough to feel acutely the meanness of its own typical experience, but powerless to transcend it'.[2]

This political awareness did not extend itself to the commercial theatre. In both form and content it remained relentlessly conservative. Experimental vitality was largely confined to small left theatre groups like Unity and to amateur theatre. Their work with agitprop, with techniques like the Living Newspaper and with plays from America was notable and was to bear fruit in the fifties, but the barrier between them and the West End was rigid. Writers like Auden tried to find a stage language but plays like *The Dog Beneath the Skin* really served only to show how far the British theatre lagged behind Europe in finding vital new forms for political expression on a large scale. There was no cross-fertilisation between the commercial and the experimental. No writers of note emerged as they had done in the United States to confront the depression and achieve box office success, like the work of Kaufman and Hart which retained an aggressive edge while making it on Broadway.

On the whole, the theatre that Coward worked in was geared to reassurance. 'Experiment' in the West End meant something like J. B. Priestley's games with time rather than the work of Brecht or Piscator; few playwrights challanged the existing order of things; Shaw had written a few experimental squibs, but no major play since *St. Joan* had beaten *The Vortex* to the title of Best Play of 1924. O'Casey remained a disturbing presence over the water, never fully assimilated or appreciated by England or Ireland. The world presented was safe, unchanging and decent. There were farces, enlivened by Robertson Hare; thrillers, in which the criminal was always brought to justice in the end: Edgar Wallace was at his most prolific when he died in 1932; there were comedies, often pale imitations of Coward; he started a vogue for plays about squabbling divorcees with *Private Lives*; *Hay Fever* sporadically generated impossible families like the one in *George and Margaret*. There were countless historical dramas, dedicated to the belief that our ancestors were just ourselves in fancy dress, from *Richard of Bordeaux* in the Middle Ages to *The Barretts of Wimpole Street* in the nineties. And most reassuring of all, there were musicals; a yearly dose of Ivor Novello provided, as the *Observer* noted, all the comforting sameness of a family Christmas, with, in consequence, 'a bloated species of relief . . . that this occasion is over for another year'.[3] It was not, in fact, one of the great eras of British playwrights and apart from the major Coward comedies the tone of it might be summed up as 'safely enjoyable'. The real sparkle and genius of the theatre lay in its actors: Gielgud and Olivier, Evans and Guinness in Shakespeare; the Aldwych farce team; the emerging and powerful presence of British ballet; and, of course, the partnership between Coward and Gertrude Lawrence.

Coward was fairly comfortable within the bounds of the Theatre of Reassurance. He could shock, surprise and win over his public; *Private Lives* provoked controversy as well as providing entertainment and *Design for Living* ran into problems with the censor which he might have expected. On the whole, however, he spent the thirties and forties wooing his public with a triple attack on the box office: through musicals, through politically comforting versions of recent history, and through plays which celebrated the virtue demanded of Emlyn Williams in *Tunnel Trench* – emotional restraint.

The British musical of the thirties and forties was a shadowy relation of the Teutonic fantasies of Romberg and Lehar. The 'yearly Novello' invariably centred on love and romance in an exotic setting which gave scope for luxurious set-pieces. There was a gipsy wedding in *Glamorous Night*, a Chinese Temple Scene costumed entirely in white in *Careless Rapture*. The music was generally lyrical, lush, relying heavily on waltzes, although a jazz or blues number might creep in. If real life intruded into the story it was tastefully sanitised; *The Dancing Years* showed a noble composer standing up against the Nazis, with all specific references to Hitler carefully removed. There was a general enthusiasm for monarchy and its implied values: the queen in *Glamorous Night* behaved exactly as Edward VIII failed to do and renounced her true love for the sake of the throne and duty.

However, in 1928 this fragile confectionery sustained a body-blow with the London opening of *Showboat*. From henceforth the American musical was to be the eternal competitor against which the British musical would struggle and generally lose. *Showboat* ran to packed houses for several years and set a new kind of pattern. It was, inevitably, a love story but it also did a good deal more: it confronted, albeit in a rather saccharine fashion, a politically sensitive issue, a marriage between races; it was also a definite celebration of certain aspects of American culture. Although showboats were a thing of the past, the black music they played was alive in the jazz and the blues of the twenties; and the story rejoiced in the capitalist vitality of the new world, showing a heroine climbing to the top of the theatrical profession and raising a child to better her own achievements while her 'gentleman' husband gambled and drank his opportunities away. It allowed characters to define themselves in relation to society as a whole through the songs that they sang ('I am' and 'I want' are recurring song themes in most American musicals); it let them sing about passion while the British musical restricted itself to an orchestrated peck on the cheek. Above all, it was an expression of community, classless and ebullient despite its sharp eye on the box office. It set the tone for the American musical throughout the thirties and beyond, a tone of optimism in the face of depression rather than the romantic escapism of its British counterpart.

Coward's stroke of box office genius in *Bitter-Sweet* was to create a synthesis; he extracted the most popular aspects, both narrative and musical, from native and American musicals and allowed them to engage in a fruitful conflict. The inspiration for the play was a new recording of *Die Fledermaus*, and its driving force a romantic reaction to the cynical sexuality of the twenties:

> The uniforms, bustles, chandeliers and gas-lit cafés all fell into place eagerly, as though they had been waiting in the limbo for just this cue to enter . . . it seemed high time for a little romantic renaissance.[4]

He was certainly successful in promoting a fashionable nostalgia: the play had an immediate effect on the clothes of its audience – hemlines dropped like conkers in autumn – and reversed the current tendency of stage musicals to employ a dance-band orchestration, heavy on the rhythm section and light on the strings. But the play did not simply return to pre-American days; it confronted the new developments and made its own statement about them.

Although *Bitter-Sweet* centres on a Viennese café of the eighteen-eighties, it opens with people dancing to jazz in 1929. An engaged couple, stuffy Henry and vivacious Dolly, quarrel across the syncopated chaos; he leaves, and we discover that she is in love with the penniless jazz pianist. Their embrace is interrupted by the elderly Lady Shayne. Coward deftly establishes her as a sympathetic character who stands for old values in a changing world:

LADY SHAYNE: So you're a musician – an amiable, sensitive looking young man – and you've been making love to this child – or has she been making love to you? – everything seems to have changed round lately.

VINCENT: It just happened – we – at least that is – I don't know.

LADY SHAYNE: Are you a married man?

VINCENT: No – of course not.

LADY SHAYNE: Well, you needn't be so vehement. I merely thought you might have forgotten –

VINCENT: My intentions are quite honourable, if presumptuous.

DOLLY: Are you angry?

LADY SHAYNE: Not in the least, my dear. What do you intend to do?

DOLLY: I don't know.

LADY SHAYNE: Well, if I were you I should make up my
mind. *SHE TURNS TOWARDS THE SUPPER
ROOM*
DOLLY: You *are* angry.
LADY SHAYNE: I detest indecision.

She is charming, but also tough, morally stronger than the
dithering Dolly. These values are identified with musical
style. Vincent, like Nicky Lancaster, expresses his rage and
frustration by launching into a jazz crescendo and the party
joins in a wild Charleston. This is cut off by Lady Shayne:

Stop – stop – it's hideous – you none of you know
anything or want anything beyond the noise and speed –
your dreams of romance are nightmares. Your
conception of life is grotesque. Come with me a little –
I'll show you – listen – listen –

The lights dim. She begins to sing, and in the dark her voice
changes to that of a young girl. When the lights come up
she is seventeen, at her music lesson with her handsome
tutor Carl. We follow her story as she leaves her dull fiancé
to elope with Carl and works with him as a singer in a
Viennese café. Here Carl is killed in a duel when one of the
customers forces his attentions on her. The story then
moves on fifteen years to find her devoted to Carl's
memory: she has made a career as a singer and is pursued
by the attractive Lord Shayne. Returning to London, she
meets her old friends at a party where she sings one of
Carl's songs. At its close she throws her flowers to Lord
Shayne; although she loves Carl still, the two of them have
clearly reached an understanding. She sings again, and the
lights change once more; she becomes the old woman of the
play's beginning, singing to the young people sprawled at

her feet. As Dolly decides to marry Vincent after all, they
take up Lady Shayne's song and distort it into a new
rhythm, Charlestoning out of the scene until she is left
alone, frail but upright, to maintain its original waltz time:

> Though my world has gone awry,
> Though the end is drawing nigh,
> I shall love you till I die,
> Goodbye!

Bitter-Sweet was an enormous success with both public
and critics; there was high praise for Coward as writer,
composer, director, and also for Coward in a new role, that
of moralist. *Play Pictorial*, often severely critical in the
past, wrote that 'It needed a man of the courage and ability
of Noel Coward to achieve the moral and artistic *tour de
force* of a piece such as *Bitter-Sweet*'.[5] The tribute may
sound somewhat quaint but it pinpoints the play's real
appeal: it is a shrewd balancing act. On the one hand the
audience can enjoy modern rhythms, the pace and energy
of jazz; perhaps, too, the touch of iron and enterprise in the
heroine owes something to the American musical ideal. On
the other, they can relish the romantic, Novelloish
escapism of the English musical in a new way. By setting
the old-fashioned waltzes and the rather trite love story in a
new framework, Coward de-familiarised them; his
audience were forced to re-examine their own nostalgia,
their attraction to old tunes and old times – and to find them
good. Instead of taking the conventional love story for
granted, they suddenly saw it as a bastion of old values,
values which are, Coward implies, not only more lasting
but more adventurous than those of the younger
generation. Paradoxically it is Lady Shayne, not Dolly and
Vincent, who speaks out most strongly for love and for the

rejection of materialism. The end of the play is almost a challenge to the American musical. As Lady Shayne sings Carl's song, *I'll see you again*, Vincent exclaims 'What a melody – my God, what a melody!' In *Showboat* the heroine's ability to make a living out of the Negro songs of her childhood is a sign of her energy and enterprise; here Vincent's foxtrot version of the song is a commercial vulgarisation, reproved by the lonely, upright figure singing the true song to herself. By allowing the traditional musical and romantic values to have the last word, Coward provided, just for a moment, that very sense of community that the British musical lacked. Nostalgia had fought the newcomer, and won.

Bitter-Sweet was, in its way, the epitaph of the British musical. From now on the American version was always to triumph both with the critics and the box office. (Many feel that it still does.) Sadly, Coward's own musicals of the thirties failed to match the brilliant start he had made. *Conversation Piece*, in 1933, a cheerfully anachronistic Regency love story, was a pretty Valentine card of a play enlivened by Yvonne Printemps and by one memorable waltz, *I'll follow my secret heart*. *Operette*, in 1938, took the well-worn theme of the aristocrat who loves a showgirl. It used the potentially interesting device of a play within a play; the heroine performs in an operette, *The Model Maid*, with a story ironically similar to her own predicament. But instead of creating a fruitful tension between fiction and 'reality' Coward merely reiterated – in what turned out to be a hopelessly confusing way – the same old class values. In both *The Model Maid* and 'real life' the heroine fails to marry her lover; the only difference is that in the play she is rudely rejected by his family and in her private life is subjected to a pathetic appeal not to 'ruin his career'. Ivor Brown's *Sketch* review described it as 'sweet and soothing' and marvelled that its composer was 'once regarded as the spirit of flaming and audacious youth'.[6]

Coward was still, over the years, to demonstrate audacity and youthful high spirits. (Tynan was to remark that he had once been Slightly in Peter Pan and had been Wholly in it ever since.) The energy of *Private Lives* and the restless experimentation in *Design for Living* were not 'soothing'. But much of his work in the next three decades was to show a preoccupation with sobriety, restraint and passion quelled rather than expressed. The subject was close to the heart of a man whose public mask was so carefully maintained. After a breakdown in 1926 he recorded his conclusion that 'People, I decided, were the danger. People were greedy and predatory, and if you gave them the chance, they would steal unscrupulously the heart and soul out of you.'[7] Alongside this concern for the public face as self-protection was a respect for the gallantry that 'millions' manifested in the face of war and disaster, for the kind of personality that was 'capable of deep suffering and incapable of cheap complaint'.[8]

If the idea of restraint fitted a part of the Coward persona, it also fitted the mood of a theatre in which Nicky Lancaster's outpourings would have seemed tasteless and excessive, where the lazy elegance of the fashionable dressing gown had given way to the hearty tweed suit, carefully made to reflect a whole code of petty snobberies about cut and style which distinguished the expensive from the ready-made, the upper-middle-class from the lower-upper-middle-class. René Cutforth once wrote a sardonic study of thirties fashion and the tense and critical stance into which it forced the body; he reserved his blackest vituperation for the Trilby hat; once a casual Bohemian response to the stuffy Victorian bowler, it had, by 1930, lowered its crown and narrowed its brim, in short 'it had become a mingy hat and there was a mingy expression to match it'.[9] A number of Coward's plays of the period tread a narrow line between restraint and minginess. He could deal with powerful feelings as long as he could show them controlled by a mask of talent and charm, by overtly theatrical skills like music or by the instinct of a natural 'performer' like Elyot. When, however, he showed those feelings at work in characters without that 'performer's' grace, the results were often wooden or unconvincing. His first attempt in the thirties to write a serious play, unleavened by comedy or music, was an unmitigated failure: *Point Valaine*, which Coward himself later described as 'neither big enough for tragedy nor light enough for comedy'.[10]

Point Valaine touches again on the *Sirocco* theme of passion for an unworthy object. At the centre of the play is Linda Valaine, a strong and independent character who keeps a hotel in the West Indies. Coward spends a good deal of time introducing the various guests, in a rather satirical spirit, and the staff, chief of whom is the sullen and brooding head waiter, the Russian Stefan. It becomes apparent that he and Linda are lovers; their relationship, however, is soon threatened. A new guest arrives – that standard hero of the thirties, a young aviator, Martin. He is beset by fever following a crash in the jungle, and as Linda nurses him they fall in love. Stefan reacts with hysterical jealousy and is overheard by Martin. Linda, realising that she has lost Martin, tells Stefan to 'Go away and die.' And he promptly does; in the last scene of the play the news comes that he has been drowned, and the curtain falls on Linda's cold response 'I must see about engaging a new head waiter.'

The problem of the play does not lie in the situation;

although this is melodramatic Coward characterises Stefan skilfully and provided Alfred Lunt with a part in which he could act against his usual charming good looks to create a brutal, lumpen demeanour that was wholly convincing. What really fails to convince is the placing of incidents: the affair between Linda and Stefan comes as a surprise curtain, as if meant to shock us – but it is not clear *why* we should be shocked. Linda's life has been shown as frustrating and lonely. Is she cynically using the only available man until a better one comes along? Or is she drawn to his brutality in some way? Similarly, Martin's jealousy is used to provide a few moments of high drama – his discovery of Linda and Stefan ensures a strong curtain in one scene and as the curtain rises on the next he is ready to depart – but his feelings are never explored. The most likeable of the guests, the writer Mortimer Quinn, sagely assures him that he will someday 'feel sorry' for Linda and then 'forget' her. But it is not clear whether Coward expects us to feel the same way. Her final line 'I must see about engaging a new head waiter' is so opaque as to be meaningless. Clearly she is controlling some kind of emotion – but it could be relief at the death of a man she has come to hate, regret for hasty words, deep sorrow for a lost lover, or indifference to everyone but the departing Martin. Potentially, the story of *Point Valaine* is a powerful one, with a strong and interesting heroine. But the effect of the play is that of a series of incidents whose emotional implications are never adequately explored. Coward later judged the characters as 'neither interesting nor kind'; perhaps this dislike of them led him to begrudge them any real articulacy or (except for the twisted Stefan) a sensuality sufficient to make their passions credible.

The response of Coward's audience to *Point Valaine* was coldly hostile. Once again, this seemed only partly due to the play's admitted flaws; there was also the usual reluctance to forgive him for trying out new dramatic territory. His next major 'experiment', however, had the perfect box-office combination of innovation and familiarity. In *Tonight at 8.30* he created ten one-act plays, designed to be performed in various combinations of three, as vehicles for himself and Gertrude Lawrence. Though some individual plays received lukewarm reviews – Coward agreed that some, like *We Were Dancing* and *Ways and Means*, were simply 'curtain-raisers' to get the audience in a good mood – the enterprise was clearly more than the sum of its parts. Coward wrote in his introduction to *Play Parade IV* that he embarked upon it 'upheld by my stubborn faith in the star system',[11] and the nine plays which constituted three nights' entertainment at the Phoenix provided Coward and Lawrence with a dazzling star showcase. They sang, danced, and changed roles with quicksilver rapidity. Lawrence shifted in minutes from the suburban shrew of *Fumed Oak* to a wickedly observed caricature of Edwina Mountbatten in *Hands Across the Sea*. Coward moved from tormented psychiatrist in love in *The Astonished Heart* to half a sleazy music-hall double-act in *Red Peppers*. Their special talents, and their unique on-stage *rapport*, were given every chance to show themselves; and the evening's entertainment was given an extra fillip from its own cheeky self-assurance in taking a unpopular and neglected form, the one-act play, and making it a success.

If the overall effect of each night was one of exuberant versatility, each one also contained a still and sober core; the mixture, in all its combinations, was essentially the same: enjoyable upper-class silliness, best exemplified by *Hands Across the Sea*; lower-class high-jinx – the Red Peppers abused each other with vigour and the censor permitted the word 'bloody' to be used for the first time since *Pygmalion*, while Coward in *Fumed Oak* threw his supper over the floor and bawled that his wife had trapped him into marriage; and a more sober and dignified piece about passion restrained.

The most technically adventurous of these was *Shadow Play*; here Coward glanced delicately at a marriage on the verge of crumbling; the wife sadly assents to 'an amicable divorce – everything below board', but she has taken too many sleeping pills and her head is swimming; there follows an impressionistic dream sequence, in which characters shift between past and present. The dream allows them to speak aloud what they have only thought, sometimes through this technique of timeslip, as when Vicky and Simon relive their first meeting:

> VICKY: You're nice and thin – your eyes are funny – you
>   move easily – I'm afraid you're terribly attractive –
> SIMON: You never said that.
> VICKY: No, but I thought it.
> SIMON: Stick to the script.
> VICKY: Small talk – a lot of small talk with quite different
>   thoughts going on behind it . . .

Sometimes their feelings are expressed through songs; the background music to their past suddenly becomes foreground, allowing them to sing about their love and their fear of loneliness and loss; isolated moments are literally placed under a spotlight and played from different viewpoints – so that, when Vicky and Simon are reconciled at the end of the play, we are aware that they have indeed learned something about each other, grown and changed.

In his other plays of love and restraint Coward relied on

the 'small talk', occasionally lifting its surface to allow passion to find a voice. This uptight 'naturalism' worked less well than *Shadow Play*. Without the theatrical devices which had brought the unspoken into the light, he was reduced to forcing out admissions of passion from characters who found that admission almost impossible, and it was perilously easy to substitute the analysis of love for the expression of it. In, for instance, *The Astonished Heart*, he tried to show love as a kind of divine thunderbolt, quoting Deuteronomy: 'The Lord shall smite thee with madness, and blindness, and astonishment of the heart.' It is perhaps significant that when the hero wishes to quote this to describe his love for his wife's friend Leonora, he has to send for the cook's Bible; the implication seems to be that in a well-ordered professional household a book so full of the extremities of violence and passion belongs below stairs. He has finally, no way of showing his love; he can merely discuss it:

CHRIS: It isn't Leonora, it's nothing to do with Leonora any more; it's the thing itself – her face and her body and her charm make a frame, but the picture's in me, before my eyes constantly, and I can't get it out –

BARBARA: Stop struggling.

CHRIS: I can't! If I stop struggling I shall be lost for ever. If I didn't know all the processes it would be easier, but I do – I watch myself all the time – when I'm talking to patients – in case I make a slip; it's as much as I can do sometimes to prevent myself from suddenly shrieking in their faces – 'Why are you here? What do you come to me for? How can I help you when there's a little brooch between us – a little brooch with emeralds and sapphires that someone gave to Leonora years ago . . .'

The moral strength of the play lies with Barbara, the wife who allows the affair to run its course and to whom her husband speaks his last words as he lies dying after leaping from a high window. But while it is possible to sympathise with her predicament and the compassionate and sometimes acid remarks which cloak her own anxiety and love –

> CHRIS: It's bitter, isn't it, to be made to put on rompers again at my age?
> BARBARA: Whether you intended it or not, that remark was definitely funny.

Chris analyses himself so effectively out of our hearts that our response to Barbara too is undercut. Ivor Brown pointed out that violent passion did not accord well with the play's chosen style – 'tight-lipped, back-to-the-audience, self-suppressive, word-swallowing'.[12] The lines, however, with their jerky rhythms and lack of flow, force the actors to adopt precisely this delivery.

The same could be said of *Still Life*, another play dealing with marriage under threat; but the enormous popularity of this play, and its still greater fame as the film *Brief Encounter* (directed in 1945 by David Lean) vindicated Coward's conviction that restraint was good box-office material. *Brief Encounter* is, after the major comedies, the one work of Coward that almost everybody knows of and has probably seen; it has featured frequently on television and its viewing figures are invariably high. Its story is that of an unconsummated affair between two married people. The play is set throughout in a station buffet, and we catch Alec and Laura, about to travel in opposite directions, at different stages of their relationship. First they meet as strangers and he takes a piece of grit from her eye; then they have been to lunch together and talk of their home lives; he describes his doctor's practice, she her husband; later, they have arranged to be together in a friend's flat, but have been interrupted and she is now suffering the torment of guilt; finally they are saying goodbye for ever and he is leaving for Africa, but a gossipy friend of Laura's interrupts their last moments. They are never alone. Their exchanges are hushed and hurried, punctuated by chatter from the buffet staff. Love, Coward suggests, changes the familiar out of recognition, shaking up the most everyday lives. As Laura puts it:

> Loving you is hard for me – it makes me a stranger in my own house. Familiar things, ordinary things that I've known for years like the dining-room curtains, and the wooden tub with a silver top that holds biscuits and a water-colour of San Remo that my mother painted, look odd to me, as though they belonged to someone else – when I've left you, when I go home, I'm more lonely than I've ever been before.

Although this is touching, there is also a sense that Coward is keeping his lovers in check because he cannot handle the energies of a less inhibited love in a setting shorn of the wit and exotic flavour of his best comedies. The film was able to create a richer subtext. Coward wrote more scenes which stressed their ordinariness – Alec and Laura watching Mickey Mouse, boating on a lake, Laura laughing at a woman's silly hat in Boots' library and worrying about the bump on her son's head, with every aspect of her surroundings making desperate passion more impossible and out of place: David Lean created aural and visual images which expressed what could not be voiced. The sound-track was shot through with Rachmaninov's brooding and romantic piano concerto, a piece of music that, naturalistically, would certainly appeal to Laura; trains, veiled in clouds of steam, were vivid reminders of the forces that brought the lovers together but would also pull them apart; Lean's lovers were constantly glimpsed in the subway to the station, a sloping tunnel whose confines suggested their closed world; one of their few visible embraces was shot in this tiny frame. Perhaps the most famous shot is that of the face of Celia Johnson as Laura tilted at a crazy angle, lit by the flashing lights of the passing express; she fails to take the Karenina way out and walks back to the buffet when it has left the station.

But although the film had its own visual beauty and provided this complex code for the lovers to reveal themselves, it, like the stage play, failed to raise certain questions. Coward, and Lean, both took Laura's return to suburban normality for granted. Her husband, dimly seen in the film and only described in the play, seems sublimely dull; Laura loves her children, but we see and hear even less of them. Nor do Alec and Laura really discuss the moral aspects of their situation. Instead, they castigate themselves. Both of them, in guilty self-loathing, describe their liaison as 'cheap', an adjective befitting the mingy hat Coward sported as Alec. To look at the script, shorn of David Lean's beautiful camera work, deprived of an audience who would automatically approve of the final sacrifice, is to find oneself asking awkward questions. A disastrous attempt in 1975 to re-make the film in a more up-to-date setting, with Richard Burton and Sophia Loren as Alec and Laura, made this plain. With no apparent religious convictions or strong relationships to keep them apart, the lovers seemed simply too timid to violate social norms or even to think well of themselves for upholding them and remaining married. Their timidity, however, fitted the mood of the thirties and forties and expressed the values implicit in *Tonight at 8.30*. The rich might be silly, the poor might be vulgar, the evening's entertainment implied: but the middle classes, the backbone of Coward's audience throughout this period, were the guardians of order, decency and the family; they could (mostly) control their unfortunate passions and come through to do the right thing. In these lively triple bills, they could even do it in a stylish context. Gênet of the *New Yorker* accurately summed up the Coward–Lawrence magic that, after all the mockery of *Private Lives*, could come down to earth and hymn respectability so well: 'Stage children, doomed to come to a bad end, and they just turned into stars, that's all. My word, what good fun they gave us. How *secure* they made our theatrical pleasures.'[13]

Through depression and war, Coward became the darling of a class very different from the Bright Young Things. He spoke for those who had managed to survive with their standard of living intact – the workers in the burgeoning light industries, the middle class who were still upwardly mobile enough to move into the new semi-detached houses that mushroomed all over the south of England, the professional classes who wanted to hang on to what they had. Coward exemplified the energy and industry they believed in, the individual success they still hoped was possible. And like them, he turned to the past rather than the future for some stable values to cling to, values embodied in a sort of romantic patriotism. The thirties saw a renewal of interest in Royalty as the guardians of family life; the hiccup of the Abdication served to point up the sensible and stable home lives of George V and his eventual successor. Urban blight and decay might be all too visible, but the countryside had hardly changed since the eighteenth century and provided a focus for a rosy view of 'England'.

Coward shared this patriotism and found a way of making it commercially successful. He never regarded himself as a political writer, and frequently re-iterated that 'political or social propaganda in the theatre is, as a general rule, a cracking bore'.[14] By 'political', though, Coward, like many, tended to mean 'calling for change'; his own treatment of history was a triumphant hymn to the *status quo*, and as such a deeply influential one.

Once, indeed, he had tried to write a 'political' play. He had considered himself largely unaffected by the First World War, which he had spent glumly squarebashing in the Artists' Rifles until he obtained a medical discharge. 'The reasons for my warped disenchantment with life must be sought elsewhere,'[15] he wrote. But by 1930 the literature of the war had begun to penetrate the public imagination, and Coward, who appeared briefly in *Journey's End* in Singapore, was moved to explore the impact of a generation's sacrifice on post-war society. The result was *Post-Mortem*, which showed the ghost of a young officer killed at the Front travelling into the world of 1930. He finds an empty café society and a hypocritical gutter press reacting against the survivors who are attempting to reveal the truth of war, preferring to mouth clichés and welcoming the ghost with kneejerk patriotic headlines: 'Return of Sir James Cavan's only son after thirteen years! His mother, a white-haired patrician lady, smiled at our special representative with shining eyes. "My son", she said simply.'

The play had some interesting technical developments. Coward boldly combined a matter-of-fact naturalism (even in scenes between the ghost and former loved ones) with almost expressionistic satire on the Fleet Street Barons. He permits characters to meet their old selves to touching effect. (The strange, stylised atmosphere may well have been enhanced by the first production of the play; never intended for performance, it was eventually staged by prisoners of war in Oflag VIIb, Eichstatt, in 1944.) There is, too, a truthful and delicate treatment of love between men. But despite some good moments, the play lacks a centre. Coward's climax is a violent denunciation of thirties complacency:

> Nothing's happening really. There are strides being made forward in science and equal sized strides being made backward in hypocrisy. People are just the same, individually pleasant and collectively idiotic. Machinery is growing magnificently, people paint pictures of it and compose ballets about it. . . . Religion is doing well. . . . Everything that isn't Love is error, like hell it is. Politically all is confusion, but that's nothing new. There's still poverty, unemployment, pain, greed, cruelty, passion and crime. There's still meanness, jealousy, money and disease. The competitive sporting spirit is being admirably fostered, particularly as regards the Olympic Games. A superb preparation for the next War, fully realised by everyone but the public that will be involved.

But the speech, like the play, has no focus. Coward, for once, wanted things to change, but had no idea how. The only answer suggested by the play is that of individual loving relationships; it closes with a farewell between the young dead soldier and his mother, hoping that by some miracle they will meet at her own death.

While *Post-Mortem* was never geared to box-office success, Coward knew that with *Cavalcade* and his subsequent historical epics he was on to a winner. He tapped a rich vein in the public consciousness about the recent past, and mined it with spectacular skill.

One of the most famous skits of the thirties, which found its way onto the stage in 1937, was Sellar's and Yeatman's spoof history, *1066 and All That*. It parodied our trite classroom view of history with the assertion 'History is not what you thought. It is *what you can remember*',[16] and proceeded to give a comically muddled account of historical clichés like the story of Alfred and the Cakes alongside repeated assertions that England was clearly 'Top Nation' despite all evidence to the contrary. The 'history' of *Cavalcade* is rather like this. Coward's equivalent of Shakespeare's Holinshed was the *Illustrated London News*; this journal recorded and interpreted world events with an eye to the picturesque and patriotic rather than their ultimate political or social significance. The numbers covering the Boer War, for instance, present it in a relentlessly optimistic light, with pictures of 'The Royal Irish Rifles' Gallant Stand' rubbing shoulders with 'Children's Fancy-Dress Ball at the Mansion House' as if every single facet of Empire was part of some grand design for the benefit of humanity. Even the advertisements shared this spirit, cashing in on current events by recommending 'BOVRIL: the energising and sustaining beverage that has been such a comfort to our soldiers in South Africa.'

Coward too treated history as a spectacle, a spectacle he brilliantly orchestrated with actors, lights and scenery, working closely with his designer, Gladys Calthrop, from the beginning of the project. The scope of his original concept is clear from the famous telegram he sent to C. B. Cochran outlining what he needed to accomplish it:

Part one small interior two departure of troopship three small interior four Mafeking Night in London music hall necessitating pivot stage five exterior front scene Birdcage Walk six Edwardian reception seven Mile End Road full stage but can be opened up gradually and done mostly with lighting part two one White City full set two small interior three Edwardian seaside resort full set bathing machines pierrots etc four *Titanic* small front scene five outbreak of war small interior six Victoria Station in fog full set and lighting effects seven air raid over London principally lighting and sound eight interior opening onto Trafalgar Square Armistice Night full stage and cast part three one General Strike full set two small interior three fashionable night club full set four small interior five impressionistic summary of modern civilisation mostly lights and effects six complete stage with panorama and Union Jack and full cast stop.[17]

Cavalcade was designed specifically to stretch Coward's powers as a director and it did so; almost all the colossal stage pictures he outlined in the telegram were realised – with some notable exceptions, the most important being the General Strike and the air raid over London. This was the 'history you can remember' – or, at least, the things people *wanted* to remember, conditioned by the popular dailies to see the most important events of the past thirty years as being those which served to unite the nation rather than divide it against itself. People flocked to see themselves in *Cavalcade*; the Old Comrades' Association of the City Imperial Volunteers packed the Theatre Royal to see actors playing the City Imperial Volunteers leaving for South Africa; many of those watching the rejoicings at the Relief of Mafeking had 'Mafficked' themselves. Coward might depict sad things – the trains packed with wounded men from the Front, the funeral of the Queen, 'an old lady, and very tired' – but they were sad things which brought all classes together to mourn. It is impossible not to respond with emotion to the precisely placed vignettes of national tragedy humanised, like this moment between a honeymoon couple on board ship:

> EDITH: . . . I don't care. This is our moment – complete and heavenly. I'm not afraid of anything. This is our own, for ever.

(*EDWARD TAKES EDITH IN HIS ARMS AND KISSES HER*)

> EDWARD: Do you think a nice warming glass of sherry would make it any more heavenly?
> EDITH: You have no soul, darling, but I'm very attached to you. Come on –

EDITH TAKES UP HER CLOAK WHICH HAS BEEN HANGING OVER THE RAIL, AND THEY WALK AWAY. THE CLOAK HAS BEEN COVERING A LIFE-BELT, AND WHEN IT IS WITHDRAWN THE WORDS "SS TITANIC" CAN BE SEEN IN BLACK LETTERS ON THE WHITE. THE LIGHTS FADE INTO COMPLETE DARKNESS, BUT THE LETTERS REMAIN GLOWING AS THE ORCHESTRA PLAYS VERY SOFTLY AND TRAGICALLY "NEARER MY GOD TO THEE".

While the audience is moved and united by familiar sights like the departing troop trains and the old songs from the First World War, they are also tacitly encouraged to perceive any disruption of the *status quo* as dangerous and leading to tragic consequences. Coward gave his story a 'human interest' by following the fortunes of two families from the Boer War to 1930 – the Marryots and the Bridges, in service with them at the start of the play. As *Cavalcade* begins, on New Year's Eve, 1900, the two families drink a toast to the new century together, but the note of harmony is not sustained. After the death of Queen Victoria the Bridges leave domestic service to open a pub. By 1906 Bridges is a hopeless drunk and is run over in a street accident, having first insulted Lady Marryot who is on a friendly visit. His wife, Ellen, is deeply distressed by his rudeness (we never see her reaction to his death) but by 1918 she too has changed. Her daughter Fanny is a well-known entertainer and in love with Lady Marryot's son Joe. After Joe has left for France, Ellen comes to see Lady Marryot about the affair. The confrontation shows Coward's perception of changing social values.

ELLEN: I found a letter from him –
JANE: And you read it?
ELLEN: Yes – it's here. I've brought it with me.
JANE: I don't wish to see it, thank you.
ELLEN: I only brought it because –
JANE: Is Fanny in any sort of trouble?
ELLEN: Oh, no. Nothing like that.
JANE: Then I think we'd better leave it until Joe comes home. Then he and Fanny can decide what they wish to do.
ELLEN: I – I didn't mean to upset you.
JANE: I'm not in the least upset.
ELLEN: It's been on my mind – it's been worrying me to death.
JANE: I think you should have spoken to Fanny before you came to me. I never interfere with my son's affairs.

ELLEN: Well, I'm sure I'm very sorry.

JANE: Please don't let's discuss it any further. Goodbye, Ellen.

ELLEN: I suppose you imagine my daughter isn't good enough to marry your son. If that's the case I can assure you you're very much mistaken; Fanny's received everywhere; she knows all the best people.

JANE: How nice for her. I wish I did.

ELLEN: Things aren't what they used to be, you know – it's all changing.

JANE: Yes, I see it is.

ELLEN: Fanny's at the top of the tree now; she's having the most wonderful offers.

JANE: Oh, Ellen!

ELLEN: What is it?

JANE: I'm so very, very sorry.

ELLEN: I don't know what you mean.

JANE: Yes, you do – inside, you must. Something seems to have gone out of all of us, and I'm not sure I like what's left.

The scene is calculated to put Ellen in the wrong. Although Fanny, in her brief scene with Joe, seems perfectly pleasant in her successful life, we are left, through Ellen, with the impression that upward social mobility makes one aggressive, vulgar – Ellen's clothes were so flashy that one review of the time seemed dimly under the impression she was a 'war profiteer' – sneaky enough to read other peoples' letters, interfering and smug. If Jane makes some snobbish assumptions (surely she would not so readily ask whether a girl from her own class in love with her son was 'in any sort of trouble') Coward engineers the situation so that she does not have to voice them in a way an audience might find unacceptable. She does not have to make overt statements of disapproval, which might alienate our sympathy, because the discussion is neatly diverted to Ellen's dishonourable behaviour about the letter. At the end of the scene Coward brings on a *deus ex machina* in the shape of a telegram from France. 'You needn't worry about Fanny and Joe any more, Ellen,' Jane tells her, 'He won't be able to come back after all because he's dead.' Then she falls in a faint.

Joe is a lay figure to us and it is hard to feel any particular regret at his parting. Coward is using his death here, it seems, not for its pathos but to avoid dealing with the issues raised by the scene; and, although there is no logical connection between the love affair and Joe's death, its dramatic placing makes it seem like a punishment for Ellen's *hubris* – an effect underlined in the film. As Jane fell, Una O'Connor as Ellen moved involuntarily to catch her, crying 'Oh my lady'. The two women were seemingly united in grief – precisely because, in the shock of that grief, their old class roles had reasserted themselves.

As the play moves into the present – 1930 – Coward creates a complex visual image which, at first, seems to hold the old and new values in tension. First we see the Marryots, once again drinking in the New Year, but they are childless and alone; Jane, however, raises her glass in a toast to 'England', hoping she will find 'dignity and greatness and peace once again.' Photographs of Mary Clare in the role show her gesture as more than life-sized, a heroic pose rather than a mere toast. This is followed by a scene in a night-club, the epitome of modernity with angular steel furniture, dominated by the figure of Fanny; she sits on a piano – a pose which at once places her literally 'above' the Marryots and suggests a casualness impossible to their dignified lifestyle – and sings *Twentieth Century Blues*. In a rapid montage which makes remarkable use of stage lighting these two tableaux are juxtaposed against other pictures of modern life – frenzied, unhappy dancers moving to jazz; 'Incurables' from the war weaving baskets; newspaper headlines flashing up in Riley lights – 'The general effect is complete chaos' as Coward put it. For a moment it seems that the end of Coward's pageant of history is like that of Virginia Woolf's in *Between the Acts* ten years later – a fragmented mirror reflecting a fragmented reality. But Coward had one last theatrical trick to play. Suddenly, the stage is dark and silent. Slowly out of the blackness shines a Union Jack, and when the lights go up the whole cast are united beneath it to sing 'God Save the King.' Until recently the national anthem was played at the end of every performance of any play in England; so, naturally, the audience of 1931 rose and joined in, themselves reinforcing the values to which Coward had given such confident expression. Dissenting voices were later, to accuse him, rather unfairly, of writing *Cavalcade* tongue in cheek, but on the whole he had established a new facet of the Coward myth, that of the patriot and spokesman for the middle-class. He had not only created a nationalistic pageant, he had reinforced national pride by beating the movies at their own spectacular game; and he had vindicated private enterprise by storming the box-office. If the solution to national problems implied by *Cavalcade* was glib and easy, he had nonetheless relieved the economic plight of a number of people – not only actors, who were paid rather more than the average wage for 'extras', but for Londoners round Drury Lane who, as the *Daily Telegraph* recorded, depended on *Cavalcade*: 'Shops, cafes, hotels and taxi-drivers all look to the show for a part of their living, and Mr. Coward himself could hardly have been more nervous than the landlady of a public house who told me success meant

£300 a week in her till.'[18] Small wonder that some people attributed the victory of the National Government two weeks after the opening to Coward. Although he shrugged that he had been lucky to have picked up that particular volume of the *Illustrated London News* 'instead of one . . . depicting the storming of the Winter Palace at St Petersburg,'[19] – that he had, indeed, been unaware that the Election was imminent – it was clear that he had precisely gauged the mood of his audience.

This Happy Breed expressed the same values but concentrated on the lower middle class, charting the fortunes of a South London family from 1919 to 1939. Once again, Coward, through his hero Frank Gibbons, extolled the supreme virtue of sticking to your station in life; those of his family who ignore this advice are slapped firmly down. His son, Reg, gets mixed up in a demonstration during the General Strike and is hit on the head; Frank tells him severely that it is no use 'a kid your age talking about blood and sweat and capitalism.' His daughter, Queenie, fancying her chances as a lady, rejects the boy next door for a bogus 'Major' who deserts her, and returns duly chastened to the family.

'Keeping your place' is the main ingredient of the quality with which Coward repeatedly attributes to 'ordinary people' in the play – common sense. While governments come and go, while Chamberlain appeases Hitler at Munich, Frank assures his baby grandson that 'the ordinary people, like you and me, know something better than all the fussy old politicians put together – we know what we belong to, where we came from, and where we're going . . . we 'aven't lived and died and struggled all these hundreds of years to get decency and justice and freedom for ourselves without being prepared to fight fifty wars if need be – to keep 'em.'

Although the generalisations are easy and jingoistic, the picture of the old man and the child had a timeliness in those last months of peace in 1939 when Coward wrote and attempted to stage the play. By the time it was staged, in 1942, it seemed inadequate as a propaganda gesture; and his portrait of the family, despite his protests that it was drawn from his own experience, has an edge of patronage, a sense of characters crudely outlined in vague generalities. It contrasts with his account of his own family in *Present Indicative*, published only two years previously, which celebrated the individuality, even eccentricity, of the Coward home life:

Mother kept on saying, 'I wonder what Eric and Arthur and Vida are doing?' and refraining from the obvious surmise that they were probably bickering like mad, I allowed the sentimentality of the moment to have its fling, and pictured. . . . Father sipping inferior port and cracking nuts and Eric and Auntie Vida wearing fireman's helmets and laughing immoderately.[20]

In 1941, however, Coward was offered an opportunity to assess, even direct, the public mood about the war. He had spent its first years in a series of frustrated attempts to use his talents in ways more important and demanding than the troop concerts and vague fact-finding missions that had been so far required of him. Now he was invited by the Two Cities Film Company to make any film he wanted, and conceived the idea of a naval *Cavalcade*, inspired by an encounter with Lord Louis Mountbatten who had described to him the sinking of his ship the *H.M.S. Kelly* off the island of Crete. The result was *In Which We Serve*, the most lavishly praised film of the war, and indeed the most lavishly praised British film ever. Released in 1942, it was chosen as the most outstanding film of the year by the United States National Board Review of Motion Pictures; it also received an accolade from the Soviet Union, where the director Pudovkin described it as 'profoundly national . . . you can see the face of the real England in it'.[21]

In 1985 this seems decidedly fulsome, for the film is by no means flawless. The dialogue Coward puts in the mouths of his ordinary seamen and their families is wooden and stilted, larded with pseudo-dialect phrases like 'you mark my words'. His portrait of 'Captain Kinross', based on Mountbatten himself, is so idealised as to emerge as a kind of cross between Henry V and Florence Nightingale. But when viewed in its context it is clearly a film put together with enormous intelligence and an understanding of how a propaganda piece should work – an understanding that, of course, springs from the box-office instinct. Coward fought to follow this instinct in the face of obstinate incomprehension from the Ministry of Information, and the fact that the script was finally approved was largely owing to the good offices of Mountbatten, himself no mean showman.

The central image of *In Which We Serve* is that of a float in rough seas, with a handful of weary men clinging to it for their lives. From this situation the story flashes back to show the lives of individual men, their families and private concerns, and the life of their now sinking ship, the destroyer *H.M.S Torrin*, from the shipyard to the moment of attack; it then moves on to the rescue of the little group and the Captain's farewell speech to his men: he tells them that although the *Torrin* is gone the spirit she engendered will fight on. Coward thus confronts the very real fear of defeat the nation experienced after Dunkirk, but contains that fear by adumbrating the possibility of ultimate victory. He frankly acknowledged the possibility of individual suffering – some of the men are killed, some of their families die in the Blitz – and even individual failure – one young stoker deserts his post in the *Torrin*'s first encounter, but redeems himself before the end of the film. At the same time, however, he stressed national unity and the strength that could result from it. The image of the men clustered around the float was a profoundly democratic symbol; from the captain to the stoker they are all tired, dirty and undefeated (no-one in this film even attempts social mobility à la Bridges). Despite the stiffness of the dialogue, the film had a sense of documentary realism: Coward gave his director, David Lean, *carte blanche* and was rewarded with scenes, such as the fast montage of the *Torrin*'s evolution in the shipyard, which had the texture of lived experience and were beautiful to look at, a celebration of the sailors and shipbuilders of Britain. His own portrayal of the Captain was quiet and downbeat, letting the heroics speak for themselves. Overall, the film was a vivid evocation of reasoned optimism, of strength gained through temporary set-backs; Coward gave his audience the reassurance of victory they wanted without insulting their intelligence. (Compare the American import *Mrs. Miniver*, depicting an ordinary British housewife capturing a German pilot single-handed in her ordinary British home, a mixture of Hollywood palazzo and Ann Hathaway's cottage.) They responded by packing the cinemas, and the Ministry of Information finally acknowledged that to show a British defeat did not necessarily have a bad effect on national morale. The Nazis also paid their own tribute, including Coward on a list of prominent people to be shot when they invaded Britain.

Coward could still fall foul of his public – for instance over his satirical song *Don't Let's Be Beastly to the Germans*, which drew sacks of angry mail from the literal-minded after it featured in a BBC broadcast. On the whole, however, the Coward myth was alive and flourishing, and its unique combination of sophistication and patriotism had a wide appeal. In the post-war world, however, it was to have a rough ride.

4
'I've Had to Formulate a Creed...'

COWARD: Would you say that this play has a theme? Does
  it illustrate for you some particular moral? Or didn't
  you have anything like that in mind when you wrote it?
WRITER: If it says anything I guess it's that one cannot go
  on living in the past and that one has to keep up with
  social change if one is going to survive.
COWARD: And is that true?[1]

The post-war world was very different from the one in
which Coward had risen to prominence. Even while *In
Which We Serve*, where every man occupied a designated
social station and did his best in it, was playing to packed
houses, the Beveridge Report, outlining a new system of
social security, was becoming a best-seller. Throughout the
war different sections of the population, through
experiences in the forces, on the land, in the factories or
through looking after evacuee children, had learned a great

deal about one another and the different conditions in which they lived. As post-war reconstruction began, full employment replaced the dole queues of the depression and underlined the importance of every working man and woman in the fight for economic survival. Society refused to classify itself into Marryots and Bridges (mostly Bridges), a refusal symbolised by the Labour victory of 1945 and the consequent rejection of Churchill (a Marryot if there ever was one) as Prime Minister. Coward was horrified. 'It is appalling to think that our Allies and enemies can see us chuck out the man who has led us so magnificently through these horrible years,' he recorded in his diary, 'I always felt that England would be bloody uncomfortable during the immediate post-war period, and it is now almost a certainty that it will be so.'[2]

In one sense all these forebodings were unjustified and the England that entered the fifties was comfortable enough for Coward. In a single week of 1951 the diary records a Conservative election victory under Churchill, lunch at the Dorchester with 'everybody there', capacity houses for his new play *Relative Values* and a triumphant début in cabaret at the Café de Paris with Princess Margaret in the audience. 'All London is fighting to get in to see me' he remarked.[3]

But despite these cheery manifestations of pre-war style, Coward was right: it was a new world, and one which he found it difficult to fit into. He had lived through many changes and had always been able to find a timely mask to fit himself; he had been Young Turk and Romantic Revivalist, Satirist and Patriot. He had had failures and bad notices, but the attacks he was to sustain in the fifties and early sixties were to cut deep. 'I suppose it is foolish to wonder why they hate me so,' he wrote after the appalling notices for *Waiting in the Wings* 'I have been too successful too long.'⁴ The only mask which appeared to be available to him was the uncomfortable one of reactionary. For the next twenty years, Coward was to find himself spelling out his ideas as to where the post-war world had gone wrong. Towards the end of the fifties, when the British theatre found itself engulfed in major changes, these were ideas about theatre; but at the beginning of the decade Coward struck out in all directions.

The theatre in which he returned to work was largely moribund. About a quarter of the theatres in London had been bombed or were so dilapidated as to be unusable. Many had turned into cinemas and the rise of television was already giving impresarios some sleepless nights. Of those theatres that remained, the majority were controlled by a small consortium known as The Group. Individuals in it had enormous power; the Prince Littler Consolidated Trust, for instance, owned Stoll Theatres, Moss Empires and the General Theatre Corporation, and Littler himself held a majority holding in the leading London management, H. M. Tennent Ltd. This meant that it was virtually impossible to get a play produced in the West End without the approval of The Group. Monopoly by businessmen was hardly the way to revitalise the theatre; their response to many of the inevitable financial stresses and strains was to sell off their assets. Theatres closed. Those still open were increasingly reluctant to chance their arm with anything not guaranteed rock-bottom success. While they did not sell out entirely to commercial interests – Binkie Beaumont of H. M. Tennent mounted some notable classical revivals – box-office interests were never far away and the West End diet consisted largely of American musicals, boulevard comedies and drawing-room dramas which contained a fat part for an established star or two. Within this atmosphere playwriting could not flourish. Kenneth Tynan lamented in 1954

> If you seek a tombstone, look about you; survey the
> peculiar nullity of our drama's prevalent genre, the
> Loamshire play. Its setting is a country house in what
> used to be called Loamshire but is now, as a heroic
> tribute to realism, sometimes called Berkshire. Except
> when someone must sneeze, or be murdered, the sun
> invariably shines. The inhabitants belong to a social class
> partly derived from romantic novels and partly from the
> playwright's vision of the leisured life he will lead after
> the play is a success – this being the only effort of
> imagination he is called on to make. Joys and sorrows are
> giggles and whimpers: the crash of denunciation
> dwindles into 'Oh, stuff, Mummy!' and 'Oh, really,
> Daddy!' . . . Loamshire is a glibly codified fairy-world,
> of no more use to the student of life than a doll's house
> would be to a student of town planning. Its vice is to have
> engulfed the theatre, thereby expelling better minds.
> Never believe that there is a shortage of playwrights;
> there are more than we have ever known; but they are all
> writing the same play.[5]

They were, clearly, writing what they believed would
appeal to The Group. The level of timidity to which the
theatre had sunk is best exemplified by a correspondence
which enlivened the pages of the *New Statesman* for much
of 1950. Under the heading 'The Theatre of Ideas', it
attracted contributions from some noted theatrical
luminaries – Rattigan, Ustinov, Bridie, O'Casey and Ted
Willis; it was lively, witty – and the debate was not about
what sort of ideas the theatre might want to express. It was
about *whether the theatre was the place for ideas at all*, a
question which one cannot imagine bothering the head of

anyone involved in the rest of European theatre and the work of Brecht or Sartre for one minute. The tone of the correspondence is defensive throughout; even the unrepentant spokesmen for a theatre consisting of 'sheer entertainment' seem bent on self-justification rather than self-celebration.

Coward did not join the debate, but his own plays during this profoundly unstimulating period reflect the predominating tendency towards a bland conformity to what The Group saw as public taste. For the first time, Coward failed either to challenge or celebrate the times he lived in. Instead he attempted to continue with the theatrical forms he had shaped to fit the old world; he could not, however, prevent a note of bitterness; even his light comedies were charged with the dislike he felt for the fifties world. As John Whiting put it, 'His technique as a writer and musician . . . became coarsened and unwieldy. He did something which has proved disastrous to him as an artist of the theatre: he raised his voice.'[6] His most overtly 'political' play since *In Which We Serve*, *Peace in our Time*, made the change apparent. Here Coward assembled another motley collection of English people – this time in a pub in Knightsbridge. His plot tried to combine a cele-bration of the Dunkirk spirit with an enjoyable dash of self-congratulatory fantasy; it shows the reactions of the English to an imagined Nazi occupation, from 1940 to a successful Resistance rising in 1945; but alongside the scenes one would expect from Coward's earlier patriotic pieces, the stories of individual heroism and humour, are a series of incidents designed to show the treachery of 'intellectuals' – implicitly left-wing – who are seen to collaborate with little or no discomfort. One of the more sympathetic characters, Alma, articulates Coward's own pet peeves in the guise of a rousing call to arms. 'In defeat,' she remarks 'we still have a chance. There'll be no time in this country for many a long day for class wars and industrial crises and political squabbles. We can be united now.' The polemic is in constant danger of overwhelming the fictitious history; it did largely overwhelm his next play, *South Sea Bubble*. Here Coward set out to create the lightest of light comedies, set in a charming fantasy world – the island of Samolo, an imaginary British colony in the Pacific. Coward had already used Samolo in his unsuccessful musical *Pacific 1860* and was to return to it as the setting for several short stories. Invariably, Samolo was to prove the kiss of death. This picture of an island where the natives 'sing from morning to night' and 'weave away and make the most lovely waste-paper baskets and never stop having scads of entrancing children', was out of place in the England that was beginning to undergo the painful process of handing over her possessions and protectorates to self-government. Coward was not even content to allow the fantasy world to remain fantasy, and peppered the play with satirical digs at this very process:

BOFFIN: I gather that this island is still a conservative stronghold?

CHRISTOPHER: On the whole, yes. There are more subversive elements, of course, but most Samolans are still Empire minded. You see, they've been happy and contented under British rule for so many years that they just don't understand when they're suddenly told that it's been nothing but a corrupt, capitalist racket from the word go.

Although staged (as *Island Fling*) in America in 1951, the play did not reach London until 1956, the year of the Suez crisis. In this context Coward seemed more out of tune with the times than ever.

He continued to mine the vein of reactionary politics and light comedy with only occasional and patchy success. His musical *Ace of Clubs* tried a new setting – the Soho underworld – but its plot was cluttered with all the devices of his more genteel operettas, and only one song, *Three Juvenile Delinquents*, had a bite to match its subject. To set it alongside *Guys and Dolls* is to realise that most of the clichés about the inferiority of the British musical to the American were certainly true in the fifties. An attempt to revisit the territory of *Private Lives* in a period setting, *Quadrille*, also received poor notices and a comedy attempting to satirise modern art, *Nude with Violin*, was reduced to a very unoriginal plot about 'masterpieces' painted by an unlikely selection of people including a small boy, a Jamaican missionary and an alcoholic chorus girl. All in all, Coward seemed to have nothing new to say about art, Soho or the Empire and was relying in these plays on a kneejerk sympathy from his audience – a sympathy that he could rely on less and less.

Relative Values shows Coward on a hobby-horse – the impossibility of social equality. Nigel, Earl of Marshwood, has fallen in love with a film star, Miranda Frayle. His family are all distressed at his plan to marry her, but no one more so than Moxie, the Countess's personal maid. Asked why, she brings down the curtain on the first scene with 'Miss Miranda Frayle happens to be my young sister.'

Miranda comes to stay at Marshwood and it is decided that to save Moxie embarrassment they will pass her off as a friend of the family; the Countess rapidly equips her with a Molyneux dress and a new hairstyle. At this point Coward tries to disarm us by anticipating some possible problems

1. *Private Lives*, Phoenix Theatre, 1930. Noel Coward as Elyot, Gertrude Lawrence as Amanda. Photo: BBC Hulton Picture Library – Sasha.

2. *Design for Living*, Ethel Barrymore Theatre, New York, 1933. Noel Coward as Leo, Alfred Lunt as Otto, Lynn Fontanne as Gilda. Photo: Mander and Mitchenson.

3. *Blithe Spirit*, St James' Theatre, 1942. Margaret Rutherford as Madame Arcati, Kay Hammond as Elvira, Fay Compton as Ruth. Photo: Mander and Mitchenson.

4. *The Vortex*, Everyman Theatre, 1924. Noel Coward as Nicky, Lillian Braithwaite as Florence. Photo: BBC Hulton Picture Library – Sasha.

5. Curtain call, *Blithe Spirit*, St James' Theatre, 1942. Fay Compton as Ruth, Noel Coward as Charles Condomine, Kay Hammond as Elvira. Photo: Cecil Beaton, copyright Sotheby's, courtesy Mander and Mitchenson.

6. *Design for Living*, Phoenix Theatre, 1973. Peter Bayliss as Ernest, Jeremy Brett as Otto, Vanessa Redgrave as Gilda, John Stride as Leo. Photo: Zoe Dominic.

7. *Waiting in the Wings*, Duke of York's, 1960. Una Venning as Cora, Maidie Andrews as Bonita, Betty Hare as Dora, Sybil Thorndike as Lotta. Photo: Angus MacBean, Mander and Mitchenson.

and putting them into the mouth of the witty and reactionary butler, Crestwell:

CRESTWELL: A coincidence in the best tradition of English high comedy, my lady. Consider how delightfully Mr Somerset Maugham would handle the situation!
PETER: I can think of other writers who wouldn't exactly sneeze at the idea.
CRESTWELL: If I may say so, sir, our later playwrights would miss the more subtle nuances. They are all too brittle. Comedies of manners swiftly become obsolete when there aren't any manners.

Although this deft self-mockery charms us into accepting the old-fashioned structure of the plot, with its pat coincidences, it also underlines the real problem of the play. Coward here equates 'manners' with the pre-war behaviour of a small group of people from a single privileged class. To an increasing number of his audience this was not an adequate definition. It might well be argued that it could be considered 'bad manners' to assume that a marriage between an aristocrat and a self-made success like a film star was out of the question. (A few years later Prince Rainier was to marry the film star Grace Kelly). More seriously, it could be 'bad manners' to assume that a servant's attempts to be like her employers were intrinsically funny. Coward seems, despite the sureness of his plotting, to be uncomfortably aware of this. In order to make the marriage seem as impossible to us as it does to the Marshwoods, he stacks the cards against Miranda. He builds up a discreditable past for her – 'she kept almost having babies but not quite', is the Countess's version of Moxie's sisterly recollections. On her entrance, she is first seen trying vainly to impress her future mother-in-law by genteely refusing a drink and wielding some uncharacteristic embroidery; then she reveals herself as a full-blown inverted snob, telling lurid stories of the 'poverty and squalor' in which she claims to have been born. 'One of my earliest memories,' she romances, 'was making a doll's house out of an old cardboard box I'd found in the dustbin.' The comedy, of course, lies in the reaction of Moxie, whom Miranda has failed to recognise; she is provoked more and still more, as Miranda elaborates on the story of her childhood with an account of the sordid death of her drunken sister: 'I suddenly realised that for the first time in my life I had failed, failed utterly. I felt guilty and ashamed, as though it was all my fault.' The tension is amusingly prolonged until the end of the second act, when Moxie at last explodes

> Poverty and squalor indeed! A London Cockney born within the sound of Bow Bells. You were born at Number Three, Station Road, Sidcup and if you can hear the sound of Bow Bells from Sidcup you must have the ears of an elk-hound!

But while he reaps his laughs from this, Coward's resolution of the plot by bringing back an old lover of Miranda's, also a film star, to reclaim her, humanises her and makes her pretences seem to spring from shyness and a sense of inadequacy rather than from real pretension and arrogance. Meanwhile, he is also sensitive enough to realise that to laugh at Moxie would be tasteless and cruel, that we must on the whole laugh with her. So he makes her play her role as family friend with spirit and dignity. The comedy arises largely from the fact that she is in disguise and can expose Miranda rather than from the disguise itself. Nonetheless, the laughs which Coward draws from that disguise are a little uncomfortable. Both Moxie and the Marshwoods almost forget the charade from time to time; she is forced to turn the 'my lady' that is always on the edge of her lips into various unlikely phrases; the Marshwoods often have to hide their surprise when she easily uses a Christian name or a phrase like 'get me a drink, I'm positively gasping'. Though the lines are artfully placed, it is no longer possible to share in the assumptions on which they are grounded; even in 1951 J. C. Trewin, hardly the most radical of critics, complained that although the play had been enjoyable, 'Once you are outside the Strand, *Relative Values* begins to fade'[7] which suggests that a certain discomfort might well have set in once the laughs were over. And, of course, the very effectiveness of Moxie in disguise undermines the import of the play. Coward has made her considerably older than Miranda; but it does not long prevent the audience from wondering what the outcome would have been if Moxie, not Miranda, had wanted to marry into the family. The curtain lines, in which Crestwell proposes a toast to 'the final inglorious disintegration of the most unlikely dream that ever troubled the foolish heart of man – social equality!' ring hollow: Coward has failed – in the post-war world, how could he succeed? – to make his case.

Coward's original audience, the people who had enjoyed being shocked by *The Vortex* and fancied Coward as hero of *Private Lives*, were now middle-aged. The theatre of the immediate post-war years was largely aimed at the middle-aged; they failed to support it. But as the first generation came of age in the welfare state, a new kind of theatre grew up to fit them. The main thrust of this came from two theatres: the Royal Court and the Theatre Royal, Stratford East. Both were committed to working with new writers and both had strong radical sympathies. Joan Littlewood's Theatre Workshop at Stratford was a direct descendant of the small radical theatre groups of the thirties; she introduced writers like Brendan Behan and Shelagh Delaney to London. George Devine leased the Royal Court with the declared intention of establishing a 'writers' theatre', and one moreover without the élitism inherent in many of the small club theatres of the last few decades. After a shaky financial start, the Court was placed on a safe footing by the success of John Osborne's play *Look Back in Anger* in 1956. Many critics compared the first night of this play to that of *The Vortex*. Like Coward's youthful firework, it showed its audience a world seldom given theatrical expression – in this case, a seedy bedsitter – and it gave the young a potential cult figure; the central character, Jimmy Porter, articulated the need of the new generation for 'good, brave causes' in the face of Tory complacency. Like Nicky Lancaster, he might be weak, misogynist and extremely fond of the sound of his own voice; but, again like Nicky Lancaster, the part was tailor-made for a charismatic actor (in this case Kenneth Haigh). Although there were more important developments in British theatre in the second half of the fifties, the most important being the impact of Brecht and Beckett, *Look Back in Anger* provided the popular press with a focus. The new drama was presented to the public as 'realistic', as working-class in origin, and as a theatre of youth. (Although only Shelagh Delaney, at eighteen, could match Coward in this respect: Osborne himself had reached the ripe old age of twenty-six.) The ironing board that featured in *Look Back in Anger* was the most photographed ironing board in history, a symbol of what the papers insisted on referring to as 'Kitchen Sink Drama.' It was publicised not only in theatre magazines and critical columns, but in women's magazines and television programmes; and, through the barrage of publicity, a new audience began to establish itself – also young, often radical, and sometimes working-class.

The new plays also demanded new acting styles. The Court and the Theatre Royal were not temples of illusion, places where their audience might escape the everyday world. Instead, they either tried to reproduce it with great accuracy, working through improvisation to uncover the emotional truth of a role and relate it to their own experience; or, as the impact of Brecht made itself felt, they maintained a cool distance from the world they portrayed and invited the audience to think and analyse it from a political viewpoint.

Both the style and the content of the new work were anathema to Coward and his diary is often vituperative, describing *A Taste of Honey*, for instance, as 'a sordid little play by a squalid little girl',[8] Osborne as 'no leader of thought or ideas, a conceited, calculating young man blowing a little trumpet'[9] and dismissing the improvisatory work of the Actor's Studio as 'pretentious balls'.[10] Suddenly, he was playing the role in which he himself had cast Sir Gerald Du Maurier, resentful of the younger generation knocking at the door of the dusbin, castigated by the press not for shocking innovations but for serving up the mixture as before, a mixture John Raymond of the *New Statesman* wrote off as 'exquisite and banal profundities.'[11] He went on to liken Coward to the floating orchestra platform in the Marx Brothers film, playing away to a receding audience across an ever increasing gulf. Coward did, literally, sail away – into tax exile in Bermuda and Switzerland, drawing yet another kind of journalistic flak with headlines like 'This unhappy Greed'.[12] It was a move prompted by his own awareness that in this atmosphere he could run dry, that his future might be a good deal less profitable than his past.

Increasingly as the fifties gave way to the sixties Coward began to articulate his ideas on theatre in a more public manner, even toying briefly with the idea of a book on theatre. He had rarely written at length about his craft; the prefaces to his published plays confined themselves to pithy and sometimes surprisingly harsh judgements on his own work. In 1961, however, he produced a series of articles for the *Sunday Times* detailing his response to the New Wave dramatists. The articles presented the theatre as 'a wonderful place, a house of strange enchantment . . . magic for millions of people'[13] and he accused the new dramatists and even the best of the new generation of actors of betraying that enchantment and thus breaking faith with the public. He attacked their scruffy clothes, their left-wing politics and their choice of working-class settings as a kind of insult to the audience, reiterating:

> Consider the public. Treat it with tact and courtesy. It will accept much from you if you are clever enough to win it to your side. Never fear it nor despise it. Coax it, charm it, stimulate it, shock it now and then if you must, make it laugh, make it cry and make it think, but above all, dear pioneers . . . never, never, never bore the living hell out of it.[14]

Coward deduced the 'boredom' of the public from the poor box-office returns; (the Royal Court lost heavily on the early works of John Arden; Pinter's *The Birthday Party* ran just one week at the Lyric; Wesker's Centre 42, which tried to offer 'a kind of pool of the best of our artists'[15] was in constant danger of going bust). In the long term, however, Coward was wrong; many of the new plays became repertory staples, the scripts remained in print for the next thirty years and Arden, Pinter, Osborne, Wesker and Delaney all had the dubious pleasure of becoming A-level set authors. If this was not commercial success on Coward's millionaire scale it still indicated the presence of an audience that was not bored.

Coward, for the first time, had begun to see 'the audience' as a homogenous and unchanging mass; the 'Public' to which he constantly refers in the articles seems to bear little resemblance to the constantly changing audience whose needs he could anticipate, fulfil, even create, in the pre-war years. He was now willing to recognise in it only the desire for enchantment, refusing to countenance the idea that new desires, new needs, were slowly evolving and that the new drama was evolving with them. When he complained of the limited range of the new actors, he also unwittingly put his finger on his own:

> Many of our greatest and most distinguished actors and actresses have come from humble beginnings . . . with determination, hard work and concentration they strove during their early years to improve themselves. They studied dancing, fencing and elocution; they banished from their speech, both onstage and off it, the restricting accents of their early environments; they trained their ears and their tongues to master alien dialects . . . to a point where they could play kings and queens, North Country farmers, foreign diplomats, Cockney cab-drivers, Irish colleens, Welsh miners and average middle-class businessmen.[15]

It is the presence of clichés like 'colleen' that give the game away; what Coward admired in this theatrical discipline was the graceful and aristocratic air it imparted, the painstaking technique that could reach what his friends the Lunts called 'the silky stage' when it seemed as natural as breathing. It is a recipe for the gentlemanly Hawtrey virtues with which he had grown up, for the stylishness that, at its best, could be seen in actors like Sir John Gielgud (who claimed to have learned most of his comic technique from Coward). But technique only solved some creative problems: it could provide alarmingly sloppy solutions to others:

> Some years ago, when I was giving alternate performances of *Present Laughter* and *This Happy Breed* at the Haymarket Theatre, I can remember to this day the relief I used to feel when, after a matinée of the former, with its tension and tempo and concentrated timing, I returned in the evening to play Frank Gibbons . . . to wander about in shirt-sleeves, take off my boots, pick my nose and drink cups of tea was so infinitely less demanding . . .[16]

The new drama wanted to find 'tension and tempo and concentrated timing' that could apply itself equally to a Frank Gibbons rather than treating him patronisingly as a soft option, a 'character part'. Coward labelled the desire 'propaganda', ignoring the fact that his own portrayal of Frank had a political basis and provided a comment on Frank's class that was no less 'biased'.

He also managed in the post-war years to produce some work which articulated his theatrical values in a way that was more oblique and hence less bitter. The earliest of these was a short story, *Star Quality*; it was written in 1951, but Coward returned to it several times, reissuing it a year after the *Sunday Times* articles and embarking on a dramatised version to celebrate his sixty-seventh birthday in 1966. Like most of his short stories, it is competent and entertaining but largely unadventurous in the way it uses the form, and is an anecdote rather than a complex work of art; but it is also a declaration – and celebration – of his conviction that great acting is a matter of instinct, not intellect, that although instantly recognisable it defies analysis. The hero is a young playwright who encounters the inevitable problems leading up to a first night – the rewrites, the squabbles between the cast – all made worse by his leading lady. Despite, or perhaps because of, the fact that she is a monster of vanity and egotism she can bring to the play a unique magic. The director of the play, a thinly disguised portrait of Coward himself, ruthlessly analyses her appeal. He rejects the obvious answers:

> Her figure and looks are little more than attractively adequate. She is virtually illiterate; her conversation is adroit and empty and although she has immense reserves of cunning and shrewdness she is not particularly intelligent. Whatever genuine emotional equipment she originally started with has long since withered and atrophied in the consuming flame of her vanity.[17]

The only explanation he can finally offer is 'star quality', which he defines as 'that extraordinary capacity for investing whatever she touches with her own truth'.[18]

Star Quality is in many ways the reverse side of the coin to the *Sunday Times* pieces. There he had praised the virtues of discipline and hard work and technique. Here these are mentioned in passing but the focus is on the fact that 'magic', or talent, or charm (the words are used interchangeably) is a rare and inborn gift, the property of an élite. It is a tribute to the star system and the style of acting it engenders. The post-war generation of actors and directors tried to work holistically, each contributing to an overall design; Coward still thought in *Vortex* terms, of 'whacking good parts' with smaller, well-written parts supporting them. The function of that painstakingly acquired technique he preached to the *Sunday Times* was to apply itself to the inborn gift and help the 'star' to exploit it.

The word 'truth' occurs surprisingly often in the story. (As it does in Coward's numerous tributes to the talent of Gertrude Lawrence.) 'Truth' is not the same thing as honesty – an attribute in which Coward's heroine is singularly lacking, lying as cheerfully to herself as to others. It is rather a complete emotional authority, the groundbase of charm. For Coward charm is not an agreeable and flashy overlay on the *rapport* between actor and audience but the essential substance of it. 'Truth' is the conviction which establishes that *rapport*, the guarantee the actor makes to the audience that the communication between them is genuine.

The relationship between the actor's charm and off-stage life is also explored in *Waiting in the Wings*, which opened in London at the Duke of York's in 1960. The initial audiences responded warmly, but the critical notices were some of the worst Coward had ever received. Robert Muller of the *Daily Mail* described it as 'Timeless, toothless prattle',[19] Bernard Levin pronounced it 'so awful as to defy analysis';[20] the only mildly charitable note was sounded in Harold Hobson's review in the *Sunday Times*: even this, however, confined its tolerance to Coward's personality, suggesting that his extensive work with theatrical charities (he was a startlingly effective President of the Actors' Orphanage for many years) gave him a kind of licence to be 'heartless' in portraying their objects.[21] In the face of all this vituperation the box office too eventually plummetted after a good start. Coward was profoundly hurt. 'To read (the notices) was like being repeatedly slashed in the face'[22] he recorded, and indeed much of his venom against the new drama can be seen as a reaction to the treatment of *Waiting in the Wings*.

Reading the notices twenty-five years later, it is hard not to feel that they are directed at Coward as a symbol of the old theatre rather than at the play. 'Noel Coward' had become a shorthand term for élitism, emptiness and all the flaws of the theatre of the early fifties. And his play was all the more vulnerable because it harked back to the theatrical tradition in which Coward had his roots and proclaimed its values.

Waiting in the Wings deals with that point in a performer's life when the instinct to charm remains, but the ability to create with it has gone. Set in a home for retired actresses, it makes no bones about the pressures that beset the final stages of their career:

> MAY: Why did you come here? Was it absolutely necessary?
>
> LOTTA: Yes, absolutely. I have a minute income of two hundred pounds a year and nothing saved; the last two plays I did were failures and – there was nothing else to be done, also I found I couldn't learn lines any more – that broke my nerve.
>
> MAY: That's what really finished me, too. I was always a slow study at the best of times, the strain became intolerable and humiliating, more humiliating even than this.
>
> LOTTA: I refuse to consider this humiliating. I think we've earned this honestly, really I do.

Deprived of the tools and techniques it needs to display itself, charm takes a painful battering in the world. The old actresses feel that they have been stuck in a backwater to wait for death. They improvise a bitter little song at the piano:

> Waiting in the wings – waiting in the wings
> Older than God, on we plod
> Waiting in the wings.

Their dependence on charity – the antithesis of applause, in that it virtually assumes a lack of talent in its object – is a constant irritation. Much of the plot concerns their longing for a solarium in the chilly home and the persistent refusal of the charity committee to grant the money. The stumbling block, ironically, is an actress member of it who, as one of the old ladies remarks acidly, 'can't act her way out of a paper bag and never could'. Eventually they get the money, but at a price: a journalist visits and against their wishes runs a story on 'these old faithful servants of the public, wearily playing out the last act of their lives, all passion spent, all glamour gone'. Later she feels guilty enough to send them a case of champagne as a peace offering, at which one of them sourly inquires 'Are we to be photographed drinking it?' The editor of the paper also pays for the solarium; but Coward places this incident very carefully in the first half of the second part, underlining the fact that it is not a 'happy ending' – merely a fringe benefit of the state of dependency they all resent. It makes up only partially for their sense of betrayal at the newspaper story, a betrayal of their dignity. 'We still have our little vanities and prides', says Coward's central character, Lotta. 'We'd like to be remembered as we were, not as we are.'

Dignity, in this play, is seen as the aspect of charm that survives even when talent has gone. The old ladies are shaped by their profession. They judge people by the standards of their former glamour – 'China blue eyes and no middle register' is the way an acquaintance is written off, while the elderly Estelle is hard on herself. 'I was an *ingenue* for years. I was pretty and my eyes were enormous. They're quite small now.' They also assert the values of the Edwardian theatre against the new. 'The Lyceum melodrama at least gave you your money's worth. An honest bit of blood and thunder's a lot more healthy than all this modern creeping about in the pitch dark and complaining.'

But more important than this, the theatre has shaped their whole way of viewing life and enabled them to carry off the harsh circumstances of their lives with grace. At its simplest level this is seen in the person of Sarita Myrtle; too senile to cope with even the restricted freedom of the home, she is carried off to hospital; but she has evolved a fantasy life for herself in which she is still a star, and her exit is in keeping with it. 'It really has been such a lovely engagement. Good luck to you all.' Those still in control of their faculties keep their sense of identity through snappy backchat that shows a player's facility:

MAUDIE: Who was it that said there was something beautiful about growing old?
BONITA: Whoever it was, I have news for him.

They use wit to fight back against dependency, and it seems odd that the accusation most often levelled at the play in 1960 was that it made fun of the old – in fact, there are no laughs in the play that do not originate with the old ladies and their sense of self-mockery.

For Lotta the instincts of her art provide her with a code of living. Coward emphasises this by the structure of the play. It is apparently casual in the way that it handles several stories – the solarium plot, Sarita's developing senility which ends in her setting the place on fire, and the story of Lotta herself; they are linked only by the theme of old age and gallantry, and the framework of the play, which starts with Lotta's arrival as a new inmate and ends one year later with her preparing to welcome another, suggests that Coward is most interested in capturing the flavour of life that itself has no real shape or structure. But on this formlessness he imposes a discipline. Lotta finds herself in two different situations which are the stuff of the old well-made plays: she encounters her rival for the love of a man she eventually married, and she meets her son from whom she has long been estranged. They are, ironically, happening at the 'wrong' stage in her life. While her actress's instinct, acquired by working in these same plays, allows her to handle both situations with dignity, the way in which they are resolved is very different from their treatment by the Edwardians.

One '*scène à faire*', for instance, is her confrontation with May, whose lover she married. Coward builds up the suspense, allowing the story of their long-standing feud to emerge piecemeal and deftly opposing May's bitterness with Lotta's graceful attempts at reconciliation. But when they finally are reconciled, it is not in a sentimental spirit; they talk quietly after an exhausting day, Lotta points out the salient fact that her husband had another mistress besides her and May 'prettier than you and prettier than me and a great deal younger than both of us.' and the conversation shifts to their shared problems as ex-performers living on charity.

Similarly the confrontation between mother and son glances at the well-made play only to reject it; Alan has read the newspaper article and feels obliged to be shocked at Lotta's plight. 'Living out your last years on public charity' he states, with guilty disapproval. Coward well knew the dramatic potential of a son railing against his mother's way of life and provides Alan with melodramatically obvious statements like 'I am your son' 'You are my mother.' Lotta gently deflates these:

> You keep on making almost defiant statements . . . You and I may be mother and son in actual fact, but spiritually we're two strangers shouting at each other across a void of thirty-three years.

In rejecting his offer of a home in Canada she is rejecting her only chance to get out of the Wings and the chance to see him; from their last embrace it is clear that she does care for him, that when she tells him their estrangement was partly due to his father's professional jealousy she is speaking the truth; but, as she says 'certain gestures are irrevocable' and Coward refuses to allow the play a conventionally happy ending. Her charm has allowed Lotta to weather her problems with grace: it is not a way of making fictions come true.

The final curtain shows all the inhabitants of the home, who have faced the loss of Sarita, the death of the eighty-two year old Deirdre, and the humiliation of the newspaper story, welcoming a new inmate with a chorus of her most famous number as a soubrette, 'Oh, Mr. Kaiser'. The jaunty tune and the frail figures make a touching curtain. It is sentimental, certainly. But it shows both knowledge and affection for the old actresses and the theatre which shaped them – a theatre in which sentiment had a place and, tempered by a performer's discipline, could be a source of strength. Coward's cast, many in their seventies and eighties, had grown up with it themselves. The play lacks the energy of Coward's major comedies, but it is a graceful tribute to a fading tradition; if he had written it ten years later, when that tradition no longer seemed a threat to new theatrical values, it might have been seen more clearly as such – not a reactionary diatribe, but a quiet farewell.

After *Waiting in the Wings* Coward's output of original plays dwindled for a few years. He composed a musical, *Sail Away*, which satisfied neither the public nor himself and generated what he described as 'an almost sensational lack of enthusiasm'[23] in both London and New York when it opened in 1962. He was largely preoccupied with less demanding projects – short stories, a novel (*Pomp and Circumstance*), film and television appearances, records, and musical adaptations of his own *Blithe Spirit* and Rattigan's *The Sleeping Prince*. But the climate was beginning to change. One of its early signs, paradoxically, appeared in one of the more negative reviews for *Sail Away*. Its author, John Whiting, had little sympathy for the show and none for Coward's post-war work. But he also recognised Coward as 'a major artist of the theatre' and suggested a context in which he might be so viewed:

> Who doesn't love his youth? For that is what Coward is to men of my age. *Private Lives*, *Conversation Piece*, *Operette*, *Tonight at 8.30*, *The Scoundrel* and all those songs we sang to our girls driving back in the red MG from the Thames pub on a summer night in 1936.[24]

By establishing Coward in the past, Whiting provided a timely reminder of his best work and diminished the effect of his present hostility to the new theatre. In his attempt to evaluate and judge Coward by his best and his worst, he also reflected a growing self-confidence in that theatre. Whiting himself had worked for some years prior to 1956 in a climate of indifference and incomprehension and had only recently risen to real fame with his play *The Devils*, the first choice of the newly-established London branch of the Royal Shakespeare Company. He was, therefore, writing with two kinds of self-assurance: first, that the British theatre had decisively changed and enlivened itself. The early activity at the Court and Stratford East was not a mere flash in the pan but heralded a new interest in both British and European drama, new subsidised companies to perform it (the sixties marked the decisive growth of the Royal Shakespeare Company and the National Theatre) and audiences drawn from the younger generations. In short, the new theatre was here to stay for a while. Second, there was an assurance that the new theatre was polymorphous. Alongside the working-class, naturalistic plays that had started the original ballyhoo were plays influenced by Brecht, by Artaud, by the Theatre of the Absurd, plays so experimental as to defy classification and plays which took active delight in the conservative restrictions of the three-act, single-set, naturalistic structure.

In this new atmosphere of confidence Coward could be re-evaluated: no longer a threat or the spokesman for entrenched values, but a distinguished predecessor. A production by James Roose-Evans of *Private Lives* at the Hampstead Theatre Club (old *Vortex* territory) in 1963 moved into the West End to reviews which reflected this spirit. 'Can it be,' wrote one, 'that we have underrated Coward all these years, and that *Private Lives* so far from being a badly dated relic is in fact the funniest play to have adorned the English theatre in this century?'[25] *Present Laughter*, *Blithe Spirit*, *The Vortex* and *Design for Living* were all successfully televised, complete with a brief preface by Coward explaining and praising the star system which underpinned them. And in 1964 he was invited to direct *Hay Fever* at the National Theatre. He wrote three new plays for himself under the title *Suite in Three Keys*, which opened in the West End in 1966 to mixed but friendly notices. Other lively revivals followed. He made some successful film appearances. His songs were rediscovered by a new generation. They suited the sixties preoccupation with style and the flip satire which was fashion's response to the break-up of the British Empire, and two song anthologies, *Cowardy Custard* and *Oh! Coward*, played respectively in the West End and on Broadway to excellent houses.

This mood of cheerful celebration continued throughout the sixties and persisted until his death in 1973. 'Dad's Renaissance', as he called it, reached its high point in 1970 with seven days of Coward revivals and features by the BBC, which he christened 'Holy Week', plus the official recognition that had so far eluded him:

> The BBC gave a terrific birthday party for me in the Lancaster Room at the Savoy . . . My birthday lunch was given by the darling Queen Mother at Clarence House . . . during lunch the Queen asked me whether I would accept Mr. Wilson's offer of a knighthood. I kissed her hand and said in a rather strangulated voice, 'Yes, Ma'am.' Apart from all this, my seventieth birthday was uneventful.[26]

The theme of a writer's reputation is the starting-point for *A Song at Twilight*, the most interesting play of Coward's final trilogy. The three plays had been planned with care for some years as 'a sort of acting-orgy swan-song'[27] for himself. His original intention had been to write a number of short plays, all set in the same Swiss hotel, under the title *Neutral Territory*. They grew longer – two long one-acters and a full length play – but retained this setting and on this neutral territory various people meet with one aspect of their lives in common – a failure to live them to the full. One play, *Come into the Garden, Maud*, deals with the theme in light comedy terms, with a henpecked hero managing to leave his wife for a continental princess before old age sets finally in. *Shadows of the Evening* shows a dying man finding a belated peace as he, his estranged wife and his mistress acknowledge a mutual dependency. Both had some touching moments, but only *A Song at Twilight* had real solidity, born out of Coward's attempts to come to terms with the theatre of his times.

It was, as many critics delighted to point out, an old-fashioned well-made play with all the hallmarks of the tradition. John Russell Taylor went so far as to call it 'the first completely convincing, completely serious well-made play in the British theatre for more than half a century'.[28] It contained not only the carefully plotted surprises of the genre but the favourite device of all: compromising letters, the secret from the past. Sir Hugo Latymer (Coward had to wait a little longer for his own knighthood) is a respected and successful writer still concerned with his literary reputation: the play opens with his capricious refusal to allow the filming of one of his novels. He is approached by a former mistress, Carlotta, who wants to publish the letters he wrote to her. He refuses, they wrangle a little and she provides the play with a classic first act curtain:

CARLOTTA: . . . to revert for a moment to the unfortunate subject of the letters. You may have them if you like. They are of no further use to me.

HUGO: That is most generous of you.

CARLOTTA: I'm afraid I can't let you have the others,
    though. That would be betraying a sacred promise.
HUGO: Others? What others?
CARLOTTA: Your letters to Perry.
HUGO *VISIBLY SHAKEN*: My letters to Perry! What do
    you mean?
CARLOTTA: Perry Sheldon. I happened to be with him
    when he died.
HUGO: What do you know about Perry Sheldon?
CARLOTTA: Among other things, that he was the only true
    love of your life. Goodnight, Hugo. Sleep well.

Within the well-tried old structure Coward was
thoroughly topical. His work on the play coincided with the
emergence of a great deal of new biographical material
about the late Somerset Maugham and Coward based his
make-up as Hugo Latymer upon him. He also wrote the
final draft while the Sexual Offences Act, legalizing
homosexuality was passing through the House of Lords, its
passage occasionally impeded by outbursts of intolerance
among some members. ('The poor old sod must be gaga'
was Coward's comment on one.)[29] While he was cynical
about the effect of the sixties' relative sexual freedom on
the theatre ('Hurrah for free speech and the death of
literature' he wrote after the *Lady Chatterley* case had been
won)[30] he was not averse to jumping on the band-wagon.
But *A Song at Twilight* tried to do more. Although he gets
his surprise curtain by announcing a theme still novel on the
sixties stage, his treatment of sexuality is more complex
than the 'plea for tolerance'[31] that some reviewers labelled
it. For Carlotta is not a blackmailer in the ordinary sense.
In the second act it transpires that she is not interested in
money but moral reparation. She has no strong feelings
about the fact of Hugo's homosexuality but is angry at his

treatment of Sheldon and angry at his dishonesty as an artist:

> But why the constant implications of heterosexual ardour? Why the self-conscious, almost lascivious references to laughing-eyed damsels with scarlet lips and pointed breasts? And, above all, why that contemptuous betrayal of Perry Sheldon? . . . He loved you, looked after you and waited on you hand and foot. For years he travelled the wide world with you. And yet in your book you dismiss him in a few lines as an 'adequate secretary.'

Coward, in fact, is returning for the last time to the subject of charm. Hugo has the same kind of emotional dishonesty as the couple in *Sirocco*, disguising selfishness as passion. He has betrayed the young Carlotta – 'You waved me like a flag to prove a fallacy', she tells him – and is now using his wife 'not only as an unpaid secretary, manager and housekeeper, but as a social camouflage as well.' But his offence is not merely a personal one. He has allowed it to make him a second-rate artist. His 'sin' is not his sexuality but a wilful betrayal of star quality, the 'truth' Coward saw as charm's necessary backbone. Moral cowardice has corrupted his work as well as his life. 'You might have been a great writer instead of merely a successful one', says Carlotta, 'and you might also have been a far happier man.'

Coward uses the twists of the well-made form to strip Hugo of his mask. His wife Hilde returns during the confrontation with Carlotta, a little merry after going out to dinner. She is singing a little song of Goethe, 'Entbehren sollst Du! sollst entbehren!', which she translates as a double edged message, 'Deny yourself! You must deny yourself!' Hugo finds this impossible as Hilde discusses him almost dispassionately with Carlotta. She dissects his weaknesses – 'He is quite incapable of recognising people as individuals. His mind classifies all human beings in groups and races and types.' She is fully aware of his sexual nature and appreciates that 'I have often been unhappy and lonely. But then so has he. The conflict within him between his natural instincts and the laws of society has been for most of his life a perpetual problem that he has had to grapple with alone.' She is even aware of Perry Sheldon, but puts another side of the story, describing Perry as 'foolish, conceited, dishonest and self-indulgent'. But given all this, she is willing to stay with Hugo; he may not love her, but his need of her is enough to make the relationship worthwhile to her. Carlotta is moved to give up the letters; the curtain falls on Hugo pensively re-reading them. In his wintry way he acknowledges his wife as if for the first time:

> *HE STARTS TO READ THE LETTER AGAIN AND THEN, WITH A SIGH, COVERS HIS EYES WITH HIS HAND.*
>
> *HILDE COMES QUIETLY BACK INTO THE ROOM. SHE STANDS LOOKING AT HIM FOR A MOMENT AND THEN SITS DOWN SILENTLY ON THE EDGE OF THE SOFA.*
>
> HUGO *AFTER A LONG PAUSE*: I heard you come in.
> HILDE *ALMOST IN A WHISPER*: Yes. I thought you did.

In this last 'whacking good part' Coward made a courageous attempt to explore his own vulnerability, to describe a predicament that as a 'star' in the mould of his own Garry Essendine he knew all too well. But as John

Lahr points out, 'whereas *Present Laughter* dramatised a predicament, *A Song at Twilight* merely states it'.[32] Much of the play consists of debate, and the debate is often stiff and awkward:

> HUGO: Your mind appears to be so clogged with outraged sentimentality that you have failed to take into account one important factor in the situation.
> CARLOTTA: What is that?
> HUGO: According to the law in England, homosexuality is still a penal offence.
> CARLOTTA: In the light of modern psychiatry and in the opinion of all sensible and prejudiced people that law has become archaic and nonsensical.

What carries the play to some extent is the relish with which it presents old age as the time when moral masks are ready to be stripped because the physical mask of charm is gone. Carlotta is sardonically zestful as she relates the end of her acting career:

> In 1957 I lost my last remaining tooth in the Curran theatre . . . it was a gallant old stump that held my lower plate together. I remember saying to my understudy one day, 'Sally, when this is out, you're on!' And sure enough, a week later it was and she was.

If the play itself had, as Alan Brien described it 'the greatest theatrical entertainer of our century desperately signalling to us that he has a message but is afraid he lacks the equipment to transmit it across the footlights'[33] Coward's own performance was a memorable one, a new way of deploying his public face. In a kind of re-run of the *Scoundrel* sequence he transformed himself from an untidy old man in a dressing gown to an elegant, self-assured celebrity in a velvet jacket, ready to take on Carlotta, 'the most elegant man in the theatre' as he appeared to one reviewer.[34] Hugo's final disintegration, all his hypocrisies stripped, served to demonstrate Coward's own performer's discipline:

> After they've sliced through his pretensions, prejudices and blimperies, he's left wordless at the end, his face working – and I mean working. The hero's a crumpled pierrot, the party's over now; but Noel Coward is in his prime.[35]

To make the play succeed fully, Coward would have needed a new form, a new vocabulary. But he did become the first writer to give expression to a dilemma that had profoundly affected the British theatre. The law and the censor had created a silence at the heart of many of Coward's talented homosexual contemporaries, a need to express themselves in alien and elliptical ways. Some, like Maugham, had marred their work with a vicious misogyny. Others, like Rattigan, had taken the suppression of feeling as their theme – a theme to which, as we have seen, Coward was also drawn. This carried its own dangers. Rattigan's work is frequently so preoccupied with the theme of pain suppressed that his plays are deprived of vital energy; emotional sclerosis becomes a kind of virtue, and real passion an object of ridicule, indulged in only by children or comic characters like the little Frenchman in *While the Sun Shines*, whose definition of love as 'a white-hot burning of the heart' is treated as a laugh line. Silence became, until the advent of the new dramatists, a potentially crippling force. The stilted dialogue in which Hugo attempts to justify himself shows how difficult the silence was to break directly. But Coward was not Hugo Latymer. He may have played safe with the censor and written some woodenly unconvincing love scenes; he may not have been 'great' in the sense of a Shakespeare or a Chekhov; but he was more than merely 'successful'; and he created, in a handful of plays, a vein of erotic comedy that was both original and truthful, as I hope to show in the second part of this book.

5
Mainly about Style

The many tributes to Coward share, despite their diversity, a common focus: his uniqueness. They may praise his plays or his songs extravagantly, they may use words like 'genius', but more frequently their specific approbation is muted, freely acknowledging that there were better writers, better composers, more variously talented actors. To celebrate Coward is not necessarily to admire a particular piece of work but to enjoy the impact of a highly personal style, the projection of a markedly individual personality upon its chosen material. Even at the lowest point in his fortunes this seemed clear. In 1953 Tynan recorded that 'Even the youngest of us will know, in fifty years' time, exactly what we mean by "a very Noel Coward sort of person".'[1] Rattigan, who by the mid-fifties saw Coward and himself as united in a common theatrical cause, called him 'simply a phenomenon'.[2] And John Osborne, who at that time cast himself as a sort of proletarian antagonist to Coward, nevertheless acknowledged that 'Mr Coward . . . is his own

114

invention and contribution to this century. Anyone who cannot see that should keep well away from the theatre.'[3]

In Coward's best plays his personality is an almost tangible presence. To read *Private Lives* or *Hay Fever* is to find yourself very much aware of Coward as actor or director; they contain clear signals to the shape and style of the action. Perhaps the best way to begin an exploration of Coward's style in the major comedies is to look, briefly, at its absence.

At present it is almost impossible to avoid seeing a revival of a Coward play. Even his less durable pieces have reappeared on the stage (*Cavalcade* was expensively staged at Chichester in 1985 and even *South Sea Bubble* put in a brief appearance at Worthing). The five major comedies have never lost their popularity and several have had recent West End revivals. This very popularity, however, means that they are not always well done. Coward is, of course, not unique in this respect. But what is significant about bad productions of his work, as opposed to bad productions of, say, Shakespeare or Chekhov, is that they seem to make very similar mistakes. There are an infinite number of ways to mess up *King Lear* or *The Cherry Orchard*: but bad Coward seems to ground itself upon one of two basic misconceptions. In doing so, it highlights the stylistic features which should, always, dictate the performance.

It would, I feel, be unfair to discuss particular productions from this point of view. It would certainly be tedious to review them all and unjust to pick on one or two. I have chosen instead to describe two imaginary composites which I will call *Blithe Hay* and *Private Laughter*.

Blithe Hay is rarely seen in the West End but can be observed with depressing frequency in amateur companies and in provincial theatres hoping to make a box-office killing. It seems to spring from a refusal to trust the play to generate its own energy and rhythm and seeks instead for indiscriminate laughter; the point of the laughter, it would appear, is not to create the appropriate mood for the play but to reassure both actors and audience that things are going well. In pursuit of laughs even mildly funny lines are signalled with a grimace beforehand and a little *moué* of triumph afterwards. Bits of comic business clutter the line of the action and tip the characters fatally into caricature. This is particularly true for the minor characters: Coward's domestics are sketchily drawn at best, but in *Blithe Hay* they sprout comic wigs, rag-bag clothing and a walk that is manically bustling or lugubriously slow. The more important characters do not escape either; speeches or scenes that are clearly designed as high points in a scene are rarely left to work on the strength of words alone: I can recall a Garry Essendine who accompanied one of his livelier tirades with a full-blown fit of hysterics, apparently unaware that Coward's term for this sort of didactic monologue (something he was fond of giving to his own friends) was 'finger-wag.'

Reviews of *Blithe Hay* often proclaim that the play is 'a laugh a minute' and this may well be the case in the auditorium if the actors are playing the caricatures well; but the show tends to leave an after-taste of irritation and dissatisfaction. The laugh-a-minute fallacy does two kinds of disservice to the play. First of all it ties down the wit to particular lines or particular bits of characterisation and belies the evanescence that is its real charm. It is, obviously, tempting to an actor to present a four-square 'character', imbued with a solid reality and emerging from a solidly conceived world, rich in mannerisms and eccentricities, a 'real person' with a real history. Coward's characters, however, are not like this. They emerge from nowhere, to embody a mood rather than convince us that they are real people. His friend and secretary, Cole Lesley, liked to tell the story of Coward's brief experiment in giving his characters a convincing 'reality' by peppering their conversation with dates and places; Lesley thoughtfully removed them all from the final typescript; for a while Coward failed to notice; he then admitted that Lesley had been quite right.

Similarly, comic lines are not there to generate a series of isolated and specific laughs but are planned to create a pattern and evoke a mood. Coward once pointed out a difficulty in playing comedy:

> It's not only getting laughs, it's stopping them. There are certain laughs which have to be quelled in order to get a bigger one later. If you have a sentence, for instance, in which there is a titter in the first part . . . and probably a big laugh at the end; a technical comedian will see to it that he hurries the first part so that they hear it but haven't time to laugh, so you get the full laugh at the end . . . if you are really on your toes, you play the audience.[4]

This technique does not apply simply to single sentences or single speeches: it is also true for the plays as a whole. They are not planned as an unbroken series of individually funny lines but as a pattern of light and shade in which laughter may be the predominant audience reaction but is invariably set off by other emotions ranging from mild amusement to sadness. Coward learned his craft as a playwright not only by working on plays but in revue; and the keynote of English revue in its twenties' heyday under Cochran and Charlot was its combination of intimacy and pace; this was achieved by the painstaking juxtaposition of the songs and sketches to give a quicksilver variety of mood. Although the overall tone might be exuberance, no Coward revue was ever complete without a song or two like *Parisian Pierrot*. It was these changes of mood within the structure that gave them their unique and successful stamp, and the lessons learned from them were never ignored in his plays.

The second kind of damage which *Blithe Hay* inflicts upon the tone of Coward's work is to undermine its particular eroticism. Its courting of easy laughs and tendency to caricature spring from an assumption typical of the 'Loamshire' play that so irritated Tynan in the 'fifties': namely, that the major source of comedy in a play concerned with relationships is the sexual incompetence of its characters. Tynan acidly remarked that English comedy of the period understood only frustrated love or hopeless *naiveté*:

> In comedies marriage is presented as the high road to divorce. Husband and wife begin the play at Daggers Drawn, their country house, and the point of the ensuing exercise is to lure them back into each other's arms . . . Among younger people the technique of courtship is even more rigorously codified. It is always practised on a chaise-longue. The girl sits down beside the boy and edges a few inches towards him, whereupon he edges a few inches away. This is repeated ad lib until the boy falls off. The purpose of this ritual is to show the English male's terror of sex and his instinctive tendency to yell for mother. . . . Until she reaches the age of thirty, the English actress is allowed only to play ingenues . . . between thirty and fifty there is a total gap . . . the erstwhile ingenue then returns to the stage, wheezing and thundering, as a dragon.[5]

The mainspring of Coward's comedies, however, is sexual self-confidence. Since *The Vortex* had created a new kind of cult anti-hero he had been quick to exploit his own attractiveness. He blandly assured an interviewer on his sixtieth birthday that 'Stardom['s] principal components are vitality and sex appeal. I am very conscious of my own sex-appeal. It is the duty of a star in my class, playing more or less myself, to be attractive to the public. The members of the audience must (not necessarily consciously) want to go to bed with me.'[6]

There is, of course, an element of bravado here and Coward presumably never wanted an audience so lovelorn that it couldn't relish his barbed one-liners. But it does show clearly that the plays must be rooted in the aura of sexual assurance that envelops his central characters, and this has consequences for the figures that surround them. Coward was concerned that they should not appear so naive or charmless as to make it incredible that they could be drawn into the orbit of his heroes in the first place. Although, for instance, he was aware of his 'dastardly and conscienceless' behaviour towards Victor and Sybil in *Private Lives*, creating 'poor things . . . little better than ninepins, lightly wooden, and only there at all to be repeatedly knocked down and stood up again'[7] he was careful to cast them with actors who were not wooden and looked capable of attracting Elyot and Amanda – Laurence Olivier and Adrienne Allen. They are perhaps his most stodgy minor characters, but even they are endowed with flashes of spirited malice to enliven them:

AMANDA: Heaven preserve me from nice women!
SYBIL: Your own reputation ought to do that.

We are rarely invited to laugh at characters, rather than at the situations in which they find themselves, and certainly not to laugh at them all the time. Where Coward does show comic *naiveté*, it is not sexual *naiveté* but a more general unworldliness, and this is never merely ridiculous; rather, it's a batty innocence which carries a certain authority. Roland Maule may have no manners and no talent for writing, but manages to spend a great deal of time with Garry and to derive pleasure from the fact; Madame Arcati's girlish enthusiasm for life and her calling are funny, but they also throw Charles Condomine's selfishness into relief and make her a fitting instrument to punish his smugness. 'A laugh a minute' is not an adequate response to the plays and a production style which tries to achieve them is not a fit style for Coward.

The besetting sin of *Private Laughter* is quite different. This kind of production occurs in the West End, or on television – in a theatrical environment where there is plenty of money to spend. Technically its standards are higher than those of *Blithe Hay* and it usually involves some star actors. The fallacy on which it is grounded, however, is that Coward is 'camp.' 'Camp' is a word so endlessly defined and re-defined that it is in danger of becoming meaningless. Sontag and Isherwood are the most eminent of the countless critics who have tried to explore the idea; plenty of critics have failed; but the term is so often applied to Coward that it is virtually unavoidable and this chapter will attempt to examine some of its implications.

Two facets of the term are most widely discussed. One of them was defined by Isherwood in his novel *The World in the Evening*, in which an expatriate Englishman comes to terms with himself and his sexuality; he is offered a notion of 'camp' as 'expressing what's basically serious to you in terms of fun and artifice.'[8] This clearly fits the spirit in which Coward invites us to 'pity the poor philosophers' in *Private Lives*, or the detachment with which Garry Essendine deploys his offstage charm, and this aspect of 'camp' will be discussed later in this chapter. But *Private Laughter* expresses another side of the coin. 'Camp's' commitment to frivolity can slip into a commitment to the second-rate. By choosing to express itself through trivia it challenges the *bourgeois* values of industry and sobriety; but instead of embracing the anarchy of this stance it tries to ingratiate and curry favour by being 'amusing'. Mark Booth defined this aspect succinctly:

> Camp is primarily a matter of self-preservation rather than sensibility. If you are alone and bored at home and in desperation you try to amuse yourself by watching an awful old film, you are not being camp. You only become so if you subsequently proclaim to others that you thought Victor Mature was divine.[9]

This stance celebrates 'good bad art'; sometimes the celebration is conducted in a spirit of amused affection; sometimes, however, it implies a bored contempt, a sneering acknowledgement that because existence is meaningless one might as well embrace the second-rate as anything else. It is in this spirit that *Private Laughter* presents Coward. Its distinguishing features are visible in the attitude of the actor to his or her role and to the characters.

There is, first of all, a certain kind of detachment which virtually amounts to parody, an attitude to the role which signals to the audience 'Look at me in this Noel Coward play, isn't it amusing?' It is frequently visible in the actors of considerable stature who appear in *Private Laughter*; the effect of slight condescension is underlined by the fact that they are often rather older than the characters they play, heightening the distance between actor and role. Coward was to complain of this as early as 1949, when *Fallen Angels*

121

was revived as a 'period piece', to be parodied rather than played as written, by actresses who were not credible as the silly young flappers he had originally conceived. This 'period piece' effect in *Private Laughter* is reflected in sets and costumes which satirise the eccentricities of the twenties and thirties rather than simply reflecting them. And, most disastrously, it creeps into the diction of the actors. Instead of finding a way of presenting Coward's speech rhythms natural to the second half of the twentieth century they resort to an imitation or parody of his own voice.

It was, in its own time, a voice uniquely capable of dealing with those rhythms; Coward had imposed upon his Teddington vowels an accent so cut-glass correct that it had a slight unreality. It gave his speech the extreme precision melting imperceptibly into irony which one often detects in the English of a highly educated non-native speaker; it fitted, admirably, the comic technique that depended on the placing and context of lines rather than jokes or epigrams. But it belonged to its own time and bore a definite relationship to contemporary educated speech. You have only to listen to a British film of the thirties or even the fifties to realise that voices have changed; our received pronunciation is less clipped, less precise, less determined to mark itself off from regional variations. To retain the Coward accent – and too many notable actors have mewed and drawled their way through the parts he created for himself – is to impose a false exoticism, an extra detachment that is not true to the spirit of the role.

Private Laughter assumes that the central characters' frivolity is grounded in boredom; 'camp' is identified with weariness and languor. Lines emerge charged with exhaustion, from bodies which lounge and sprawl, albeit elegantly, as if the prospect of moving were too painful to contemplate. The frequent quarrels between characters become expressions of a general misanthropy and the lovemaking a kind of emotional slumming, a psychic equivalent of 'good bad art' without even the relish that implies. If *Blithe Hay* courts reviews which pronounce it 'a laugh a minute', *Private Laughter* seeks for epithets like 'elegant' and 'bitchy' – words Coward did not necessarily regard as praise. He took considerable exception to an American production of *Present Laughter* which portrayed Garry Essendine as waspish and languidly cruel; and his succinct comment to a young actress playing Amanda in the 'camp' style she had associated with the Coward image was 'too piss-elegant by half'.

Coward is not the only writer to suffer from this kind of delivery; it tends to appear in Wilde, in Restoration Comedy, in any play which might be termed a comedy of manners. The late Joe Orton, who found much of his own work treated as 'camp', put his finger firmly on one of the chief fallacies that lie behind it: the belief that 'style' is a kind of patina which overlays the comedy rather than an organic part of it:

The style isn't superimposed. It's me. You can't write stylised comedy in inverted commas, because the style must ring of the man, and if you think in a certain way you write true to yourself . . . style isn't camp or chi-chi. I write in a certain way because I can't express certain things in naturalistic terms . . . Oscar Wilde's style is much more earthy and colloquial than most people notice. When we look at Lady Bracknell, she's the most ordinary, common, direct woman; she's not an affected woman at all. People are taken in by the 'glittering style.' It's not glitter. Congreve is the same. It's real – a slice of life. It's just very brilliantly written, perfectly believable. Nothing at all incredible.[10]

Wilde's language is perfectly structured; the characters all speak in sentences that could serve as grammar-book examples, and, of course, with considerable wit. But alongside the wit there are, as Orton points out, very 'earthy' concerns, the pursuit of marriage for both love and money. Virtually all comedy, from *Tom and Jerry* to *The Winter's Tale*, is essentially concerned with survival, whether on the most basic level of life itself or in terms of preserving a psychic wholeness and harmony with nature. Wilde, like the playwrights of the Restoration, is concerned with survival in a certain section of society; his characters struggle to remain not just alive and free but acceptable at Society balls and with unlimited credit at Coutts.

For both Wilde and his comedic forebears part of the survival strategy was an apparently ordered family life, marriage into the desirable social class and its subsequent preservation. Wilde's disregard of the convention in real life proved fatal to him. For the world in which Coward grew up, stable marriage was ceasing to become a vital element in this social survival. Divorce might make it impossible to be received at Court, but it was no longer unthinkable – at least, not for the wealthy, many of whom could echo Elyot Chase's experience: 'I spent a whole week-end at Brighton with a lady called Vera Williams. She had the nastiest looking hairbrush I have ever seen.'

But if marriage is no longer a goal for Coward's characters, there are still 'earthy' concerns with survival which energise their behaviour just as the pursuit of sex-with-a-dowry energises that of Ernest and Algy and the Restoration rake; Elyot and Garry and Gilda and the

Blisses are not trying to achieve money or love, but to hang on to the lifestyle they already have. All have carefully constructed masks, techniques for using their charm to best advantage, and have to defend them in the face of threats; the threats may be from without, as in *Hay Fever* and *Present Laughter*, where the less stylish people in their world try to batten on their energy and sex-appeal; or they may be from within, as in *Private Lives* and *Design for Living*, where the very intensity of their own feelings can knock the carefully constructed persona flying; they may even be from both sides, as in *Blithe Spirit*. But they are all powerful enough to force Coward's characters to struggle to keep their territory from slipping beneath their immaculately stylish feet, and in doing so create considerable energy.

André Charlot, directing the first revue for which Coward had prime responsibility, *London Calling!*, evolved a method of obtaining the speed and pace he desired from the cast: he put on a matinée just before the opening, so that they played to the first-night critics with a fierce energy born of total exhaustion. This edgy vitality is the most appropriate spirit in which to play the major comedies. It brings out the side of them that is 'camp' in the sense Isherwood described of expressing serious feelings in terms of a joke; or, as Susan Sontag put it, their 'state of continual incandescence . . . being one very intense thing'.[11] For the Coward character, ego is all. There is not much else to believe in:

ELYOT: You have no faith, that's what's wrong with you.
AMANDA: Absolutely none.
ELYOT: Don't you believe in –? *HE NODS UPWARDS*
AMANDA: No, do you?

ELYOT *SHAKING HIS HEAD*: No. What about –? *HE POINTS DOWNWARDS*

AMANDA: Oh dear no.

ELYOT: Don't you believe in anything?

AMANDA: Oh yes, I believe in being kind to everyone, and giving money to old beggar women, and being as gay as possible.

ELYOT: What about after we're dead?

AMANDA: I think a rather gloomy merging into everything, don't you?

ELYOT: I hope not, I'm a bad merger.

This is as precise as any Coward character ever manages to be on the forces that shape most people's lives – religion, politics, money, work, children, hunger. But within the charmed circle of selfishness they live intensely; they blossom when this selfishness is understood, react with rage when expected to abandon it:

AMANDA: . . . I won't make any difficulties. I'll go away, far away, Morocco, or Tunis, or somewhere. I shall probably catch some dreadful disease, and die out there, all alone – oh, dear!

VICTOR: It's no use pitying yourself.

AMANDA: I seem to be the only one who does. I might just as well enjoy it.

It is this selfishness, this intense commitment to the ego and its right to express itself in the face of all appeals to be more reasonable, more aware of reality, more *ordinary*, that brings the plays to life. John Lahr wrote 'the characters are grown-up adolescents. There is no family life to speak of, no children, no commitment except to pleasure . . . they appeal to the audience because their frivolity has a kind of stoic dignity.'[12]

This 'dignity' arises from the fact that they keep their heads – or masks – above water at considerable cost. Most of their predecessors in Wilde or Congreve had, despite the energy of their plots and counterplots, a lazy elegance about their dialogue and movements. Coward's best plays are almost plotless but nevertheless give an impression of bubbling speed. Like the Art Deco figures popular in the twenties, the characters seem in constant motion, an energy that can be heard in the language and also clearly seen in the action and *décor* of the plays.

Every set, for instance, suggests impermanence. They are frequently cluttered with luggage indicating various arrivals and departures – by the end of *Present Laughter* Garry's flat is deep in his own trunks and boxes plus those of all the characters threatening to accompany him to Africa. Although generally attractive and cheerful to look at – Coward's favoured designer, Gladys Calthrop, used a great deal of white and strong and festive colours – the locations have a temporary air. *Private Lives*, of course, opens in a French hotel; both Gilda and Garry live in 'studios', places of work rather than permanent homes; in *Hay Fever* the action takes place on Bliss home territory, but all we see is the hall; the guests do penetrate other rooms, but always briefly, returning to the hall as if all too aware that they are not really welcome; and in *Blithe Spirit* the set is finally torn apart by the restless ghosts.

Costume, too, adds to the bustling air of the scenery; often it is also connected with travel or movement: people wear travelling clothes or, sometimes, borrowed garments like pyjamas. Often their clothes are clearly purposeful. Joanna's evening dress in *Present Laughter* has been put on with the express purpose of seducing Garry and we actually see her putting the finishing touches to herself onstage; Judith Bliss dons an eccentric outfit of tea-gown, galoshes and a big hat and carries a trug to support the role she has assumed of retired star turned country gentlewoman; but she is well aware of the effects she can make and is artist enough to remove her hat at the right moment to allow Sandy to admire her properly. The dressing-gown has, of course, become a Coward cliché; but it is worth examining its role in the plays. On the whole, it is not associated with sleep or even rest; it connotes informality, vanity (Garry has eighteen, all different and very bright) luxury and above all freedom of movement. Coward was a close friend of the designer Edward Molyneux; as with Gladys Calthrop, he used his designs both onstage and off, and they were often an integral part of his work from the beginning. His first inkling of *Private Lives*, for instance, was a mental picture of 'Gertie (Lawrence) . . . in a white Molyneux dress on a terrace in the South of France'.[13] The dress, like most of the other designs Molyneux did for Coward, expressed wealth and good taste, but it also flowed gracefully and allowed the wearer to run or kick if she chose. The dressing-gowns were an extension of this freedom; if most Molyneux designs were reminiscent of sportswear, the dressing-gowns, or the pyjamas like the flame-coloured one-piece worn in the second act of *Private Lives*, went a stage further; they are play clothes, an adult version of the romper suit. Their wearers play games, throw tantrums and roll on the floor fighting. They suggest simultaneously a childish sensibility and an acceptance of the fact in dressing for this sort of activity. Coward's central characters may make fools of themselves, but at least they dress the part and their self-assurance in this respect can make others look silly by contrast: in *Private Lives*, for instance, Victor and Sybil arrive at Amanda's flat in smart travelling suits which are rumpled and uncomfortable after they have been forced to spend the night on sofas, in marked contrast to the at-home comfort of the other pair; Joanna's evening clothes look draggled and inappropriate the morning after and underline the fact that she has no real place in 'the firm' that looks after Garry's interests.

The physical stance the carefully specified clothes demand is that required by a favourite activity of the twenties, tap dancing. It is simultaneously relaxed and disciplined, capable of energy and precision. The action of the plays is far more physically strenuous than an account of the plots would suggest. Although not much happens in a Coward play, compared to the well-made dramas that preceded him, there is a great deal of activity. People sing, dance, fight; when they have long speeches they frequently utter them while pacing about like caged tigers. From time to time they embrace. Onstage kisses usually make for some slight slackening of pace and tension, but in Coward they tend to generate even more energy. They may turn rapidly into vigorous quarrelling, as in *Private Lives*; they may provide a brisk climax to a scene of agonised self-examination; in *Design For Living*, for instance, Otto and Gilda suddenly stop debating the rights and wrongs of their affair as he vaults the sofa crying 'How do you do?' in Norwegian. This technique of undercutting the kiss with a totally irrelevant line is also common; most embraces in Coward are the prelude to a laugh line and are placed as such; it is almost impossible to insert any kind of caress not demanded by the text without spoiling the line of the action.

Blows are placed with equal care and happen with greater frequency. They rarely come as a surprise – the fight between Elyot and Amanda is built up verbally with great care – and their comic effect is more complex than the rather slapstick nature of the gesture would seem to allow. In *Present Laughter*, for instance, Joanna slaps Garry very close to the final curtain; for a few seconds it looks like the comic climax of the play, with Joanna looking ridiculous for the fury of her preliminary tirade and Garry even more ridiculous on the receiving end of the slap. But the laugh comes from the fact that it isn't the climax; Garry, whose lovemaking has hitherto been permanently imbued with the sense of 'watching myself go by' has at last forgotten himself, wholly absorbed in his fury at being contracted to a theatre he dislikes. The slap is totally ignored as he turns on his staff for booking 'an auditorium that looks like a Gothic edition of Wembley Stadium.' Characteristically, Coward gets his laugh by allowing his hero to remain himself in the face of chaos; as with cartoon characters, our pleasure lies in the fact that these people do not grow up or develop; they remain their appalling selves.

The language of the plays similarly expresses the stasis of these monstrous egos and the energy needed to preserve it. If the clue to the physical behaviour of the Coward actor lay in dance, the key to the verbal skills needed lies in Coward's songs and revue sketches. Coward never saw himself as a major composer, simply as a creator of 'pleasant sounds', but when Elyot remarked in *Private Lives* on the potency of cheap music he spoke for his generation. Snatches of songs, imitation jazz lyrics pervade the poems of Auden and MacNeice, are quoted throughout novels like *Brighton Rock* and *Stamboul Train*. Coward's facility made him a popular revue artist; but it also shaped his prose and imposed rhythms for the actor to follow. In his more sentimental songs, like *I'll See You Again* or the 'nasty insistent little tune' that dogs Elyot, *Someday I'll Find You*, the waltz rhythm is very marked, in the old-fashioned Viennese style rather than the style of the thirties, and it governs the scenes in which it appears. In *Private Lives* the repeated intrusion of the orchestra forces Elyot and Amanda away from flippancy and quick exchanges:

> AMANDA: Have you known her long?
> ELYOT: About four months, we met in a house party in Norfolk.
> AMANDA: Very flat, Norfolk.
> ELYOT: How old is dear Victor?
> AMANDA: Thirty-four, or five; and Sybil?
> ELYOT: I blush to tell you, only twenty-three.
> AMANDA: You've gone a mucker alright.

into gentler rhythms:

> ELYOT: You always had a sweet voice, Amanda.
> AMANDA: Thank you.
> ELYOT: I'm awfully sorry about this, really I am. I wouldn't have had it happen for all the world.

The pace of the dialogue reflects the increasing closeness of the lovers as they move towards one another, withdraw as the music ends, draw together as it starts again and finally end in each other's arms.

The comic songs too contain the key to the speaking of Coward's lines. Like the longer speeches, they are grammatically very precise and far more complex in their sentence structure than those of most noted song-writers; instead of a series of simple sentences linked by the occasional 'and' or 'but', they pile up subordinate clauses:

> It's such a surprise for the Eastern eyes to see
> That though the English are effete,
> They're quite impervious to heat,

131

When the white man rides every native hides in glee
Because the simple creatures hope he
Will impale his solar topee on a tree.
                              (*Mad Dogs and Englishmen*)

Coward once styled himself 'one of the few remaining
guardians of the English language'[14] but the impression
given by this grammatical accuracy is not so much of
precision as of extreme self-confidence; the world may be
slipping from under the feet of Coward's characters but it
does not interfere with their ability to express themselves.
They are fuelled for their quarrels and complaints against
the hostile world by the springing rhythms of his prose; the
kind of delivery Coward expects can be clearly seen in the
songs by the way in which he distributes rhyme. It will
strike, not just at the end of the line where the singer can
take a breath, but in the middle, where he can only take the
briefest break:

The India that one reads about
And may have been misled about
In one respect has kept itself intact.
Though 'Pukka Sahib' traditions may have cracked
And thinned
The good old Ind-
                              ian army's still a fact.
That famous monumental man
The Officer and Gentleman
Still lives and breathes and functions from
                              Bombay to Katmandu.
                              (*I Wonder What Happened to Him?*)

The effect of the break is not simply to point up a comic
rhyme but to push the singer on to finish the next section

without another breath. A similar kind of energising effect is obtained by his habit of throwing away a comic line, placing it outside the pattern of the rhyme:

> The Stately Homes of England
> We proudly represent,
> We only keep them up for
> Americans to rent.
> Though the pipes that supply the bathroom burst
> And the lavatory makes you fear the worst
> It was used by Charles the First
> Quite informally . . .
>
> (*The Stately Homes of England*)

In fact, most of Coward's verbal strategies are designed to promote speed of delivery. In his cabaret act of the fifties – described by Tynan as the best way 'to see him whole, public and private personalities conjoined'[15] – he delivered the well-known numbers with the speed of a machine-gun. His rendering of *Mad Dogs and Englishmen* grew faster every year; late recordings (although every word is audible) suggest that the performance is almost an in-joke with the audience, the focus shifted from the lines themselves to Coward's record-breaking delivery.

Nevertheless, it comes as a shock to hear the recordings that Coward made with Gertrude Lawrence of the most famous scene in *Private Lives*. The lines are generally delivered laden with pauses to convey the subtext, the emotion beneath the trivial topics:

AMANDA: What have you been doing lately? During these last years?

ELYOT: Travelling about. I went round the world, you know, after –

AMANDA: Yes, yes, I know. How was it?

ELYOT: The world?
AMANDA: Yes.
ELYOT: Oh, highly enjoyable.
AMANDA: China must be very interesting.
ELYOT: Very big, China.
AMANDA: And Japan –
ELYOT: Very small.

Lawrence and Coward, by contrast, spoke them briskly, each capping the other's line without a pause. There seems, at first hearing, almost no room for emotion. But it soon becomes clear that the speed is not a mere idiosyncrasy but reinforces an important aspect of the characters: their attitude to language. It is an attitude they share with Coward: language is a performer's instrument, a tool for charm; used accurately, it can carry any kind of emotional weight.

Coward's relish for words can be seen in his earliest comic pieces. He had a sharp ear for silliness or eccentricity. Although he was not self-effacing enough to write good parodies of particular artists (his famous Sitwell skits are not very convincing) he deftly captured the tone of the more pretentious varieties of popular literature; *A Withered Nosegay* tilted cheerfully at the sugary historical romances of the twenties – 'The day of her execution dawned fair over St Paul's Cathedral. Sophie in her little cell rose early and turned her *fichu*'.[16] The pseudo-historicism of that anachronistic *fichu* displays a concern for the *mot juste* not then apparent in his plays; but by the time he wrote *Hay Fever* he was showing that concern as an integral part of his characters. Judith Bliss, for instance, struggles to make her chosen self-image of country gentlewoman more authentic by 'learning the names of the flowers by heart':

JUDITH: Delphiniums are those stubby red flowers, aren't they?

SIMON: No, darling; they're tall and blue.

JUDITH: Yes of course. The red ones are somebody's name – Asters, that's it. I knew it was something opulent.

A new phrase to most of Coward's egocentric charmers is like a bright pebble to a baby, something to be played with and examined and put in the mouth even if the circumstances are not very favourable; Elyot and Amanda stop in the middle of a fight to debate whether adders could be said to snap or sting; to Coward himself in the role of Elyot his kind of play was second nature and Laurence Olivier recalls an improvised exchange in the play's first run:

ELYOT: Amanda? Amanda is a fishwife.

VICTOR: Oh I say, look here . . .

ELYOT: A fishwife, I tell you! A fishiff! Tell me, does one say fishwife or fishiff?

VICTOR: Oh well . . . I suppose . . . it might be the same as, er, mid- oh. Er.[17]

This instinct for the playful in language is something the characters develop at the expense of its more conventional aspects; they are often unaware of any kind of terminology outside their immediate experience – Elyot talks about science as 'Cosmic Atoms, and Television, and those gland injections', while Judith tenderly patronises the sporting Sandy:

JUDITH: . . . Would you like a drink?

SANDY: No, thanks. I'm in training.

JUDITH: How lovely! What for?
SANDY: I'm boxing again in a couple of weeks.
JUDITH: I must come to your first night.

The effect of this grand ignorance is to make us laugh not at their intellectual laziness but at the bold egocentricity with which they define their worlds. It is Judith, not Sandy, who comes out on top in this exchange. For the duration of the play, we are forced to refrain from judging them outside their own terms of reference; instead we judge the quality of their performance in the circus of the ego and the relationship between character and mask.

This highly self-conscious use of language precludes the use of a 'subtext' in the conventionally understood sense of an emotional pattern existing beneath the words, not obvious to all the speakers themselves. Vicky in *Shadow Play* speaks of 'Small talk, a lot of small talk with other thoughts going on behind.' But the 'other thoughts' for most of Coward's characters are more or less transparent. Language does not conceal feeling but expresses the struggle to reveal it within the confines of charm. In the famous balcony scene Elyot and Amanda are simultaneously aware that they are playing a game and describing their feelings:

AMANDA: Did you eat sharks' fins, and take your shoes off, and use chopsticks and everything?
ELYOT: Practically everything.
AMANDA: And India, the burning Ghars, or Ghats, or whatever they are, and the Taj Mahal. How was the Taj Mahal?
ELYOT: Unbelievable, a sort of dream.
AMANDA: That was the moonlight, I expect, you must have seen it in the moonlight.

ELYOT: Yes, moonlight is cruelly deceptive.

AMANDA: And it didn't look like a biscuit box, did it? I've always felt that it might.

ELYOT: Darling, darling, I love you so.

AMANDA: And I do hope you met a sacred elephant. They're lint white I believe, and very, very sweet.

ELYOT: I've never loved anyone else for a moment.

It is perfectly plain to Elyot, to Amanda and to us that the talk of deception and disillusion is really concerned with their own relationship and their half-fear, half-desire that it is about to assert itself again. There is no need for the actors to overlay the dialogue with pregnant pauses or significant looks. What makes this exchange both comic and moving is the fact that it is clearly a code between two natural performers; they are looking for a way to say what they feel without abandoning their personal style. The flippancy shows a recognition of their mutual need to act out the situation with flair; for once, they are considerate of each other, and it is this consideration which makes the cues fall so pat. Elsewhere the speed of the play comes from the energy of their quarrels and their irritation with their prospective partners who do not understand this performers' need.

If the attitude to language as a performer's instrument colours the speech of the characters and energises the play, so too does their particular awareness of sexuality. They are, as we have seen, remarkably self-confident about their own attractions. But they also display an interesting androgyny.

Like most comic writers, Coward wrote about sex. In the climate of opinion in which he wrote it was possible for his characters, unlike, say, Wilde's or Maugham's, to admit to a degree of promiscuity without either losing audience sympathy or labelling themselves as tragic victims of society. But their language is invariably moderate, their behaviour onstage relatively decorous. Coward greatly disliked sexual explicitness in theatre:

> There has been a rumour floating about, secretly, that I may be asked to direct *Love for Love* at the National Theatre. I have read it and would rather die. It's no good, I simply cannot abide Restoration comedy. I am sure it was good in its time, but now its obvious, bawdy roguishness bores the hell out of me. . . . It is, I suppose, kind of critics to compare me to Congreve, but I do wish they hadn't.[18]

Double-entendre is virtually non-existent in the plays; even in the songs it is confined to the occasional, deliberately prudish euphemism thrown deftly to the listener's imagination, like Coward's slightly shocked account in *I Wonder What Happened to Him?* of 'that bloke in the Third' who 'took to pig-sticking in *quite* the wrong way.' Some characters even take pains to flaunt their detachment. Garry Essendine proclaims, after several acts of mildly enthusiastic dalliance, that

> to me the whole business is vastly over-rated. I enjoy it for what it's worth and fully intend to go on doing so for as long as anybody's interested and when the time comes that they're not I shall be perfectly content to settle down with an apple and a good book!

This kind of detachment is almost suggested as an ideal; passion itself is inconvenient, violent and hard on the nerves. 'We're in love all right', says Elyot after a particularly nasty row with Amanda, and they rapidly launch into yet another. The formal ties that passion leads to are also seen as a threat: to Amanda the fact of marriage itself was the source of her original inability to live with Elyot; for Gilda

> The only reasons for me to marry would be these: to have children; to have a home; to have a background for social activities, and to be provided for. Well, I don't like children; I don't wish for a home; I can't bear social activities, and I have a small but adequate income of my own . . . to be tied legally . . . would be repellent.

The only use of any of Coward's comic characters seems to find for marriage is as a useful bolt-hole when the rest of the world intrudes too much: Garry goes back to his efficient wife to escape a flatful of pursuers; Elyot and Amanda walk out of the new marriages and back to their old one; the Blisses are so intolerable to anyone else they have to stick together. The only happy love, in fact, seems to be totally irresponsible.

This has sometimes led to Coward's plays being seen as dangerously divorced from the real world; in Coward's predecessors in the comedy of manners, the consequences of the characters' sexual behaviour in society as a whole are always clear; the world outside is still present. Here, as John Russell Taylor points out

> Coward's drawing-rooms are nurseries where overgrown children can take refuge, safe from the world, to play at being grown-ups for as long as they care to and on exactly what terms they choose . . . all is resolved with a return to first principles: Garry goes back to Liz, since nanny always knows best.[19]

The habitual final gesture of Coward's lovers, tiptoeing away from the chaos they have caused, has been contrasted unfavourably with the clear-sighted plans for marriage which conclude the better Restoration comedies, indicating as they do some signs of real moral growth on the part of the more sympathetic characters. Bonamy Dobrée, for instance, writing at the height of the theatrical revival of Restoration Comedy in the twenties, spoke of the plays as 'attempt(s) to rationalise sexual relationships';[20] certainly the lovers who seem to be given the approval of their authors try to evolve a relationship that is less mercenary and less moonstruck than those of their circle, symbolised by the proviso-scenes in which they spell out the terms on which they can live amicably together. Beside this, Coward's lovers, unhappy together, unhappy apart, may at first seem to lack substance.

But Coward is exploring a different world; frivolous, privileged, egocentric, but still a pocket of a society, and one in which sexual *mores* were changing; and within this society, I believe, his comedies are more illuminating than their playfulness would at first seem to allow. Meredith made a pronouncement on comedy that has become a cliché:

> there will never be civilisation where comedy is not possible; and that comes of some degree of social equality between the sexes.[21]

Millamant and her kind are seen as classic illustrations of the point: witty, charming, they are able to tease their lovers, teach them manners, and marry upon terms that suit them. And yet the key word in Meredith's observation is *some* degree. To speculate on the degree of freedom that the Restoration man and woman yield to each other is to

140

become aware of yawning inequalities; the woman will inevitably become financially dependent; her lover may rise above the base mercenary motives of some Restoration heroes, but he will have the upper hand nonetheless. Similarly the prospects for a bachelor and a spinster are not equal, in status, in sexual freedom, or, unless the woman is her father's sole heir, in wealth. Invariably, beneath the jokes, the relationship between man and woman in these comedies is based on necessity – her need for security, his need for her dowry; inevitably, it is thus one of hunter and prey, although both sexes may play both roles at different points. Rarely, however do they face each other as true equals.

For Coward's generation, as I have said, attitudes to marriage were changing. In comedy it was no longer necessarily the goal or the reward reserved for the most attractive or the most sympathetic characters; it was a possibility among other possibilities. For Coward's characters, rich, independent and unconcerned with approval or acceptance outside their own narrow circle, this is particularly true; no one is forced by social pressures, religious scruples or financial hardship to remain in an unhappy relationship or to refrain from a promising one. This is hardly a 'realistic' view of relationships within society as a whole, but by removing his characters so thoroughly from the everyday world, Coward is enabled to examine their emotional struggles in a very concentrated form, to put sexual attraction under a microscope. This concentration leads him to take a hard look at conventional sex-roles. Invariably, his more stylish characters find these ridiculous; males and females are equally rich and independent and thus equally free from the pressures to conform to a stereotype, and they celebrate this freedom with anarchic relish.

In these comedies, to play a conventional sex role is to
wear blinkers. We can sense that Victor's marriage to
Amanda will not last beyond the honeymoon as soon as he
pronounces 'I'm glad I'm normal', and goes on to illustrate
his 'normality' by producing a conventionally 'masculine'
response to every situation from the prospect of a
suntanned wife ('I hate sunburnt women . . . it's somehow,
well, unsuitable') to Elyot's prudent avoidance of a fist
fight. ('Oh, for God's sake, behave like a man.') To
'behave like a man' is to be shot through with irrational
prejudice, just as to 'behave like a woman' is to be clinging,
insecure and vindictive. When Elyot remarks to Sybil
'You're a completely feminine little creature, aren't you?'
he does not mean it as a compliment. He implies a desire
for someone not 'completely feminine', for Amanda's
ability to treat him neither as master nor lapdog; it is only
when he feels at a disadvantage in their quarrels that he
makes statements like 'That is a little different. I'm a man',
and they are invariably treated to Amanda's withering
contempt. Similarly Garry Essendine – although capable of
launching into a love scene cribbed from his latest West
End success to get himself out of a difficult situation – has a
fundamental contempt for 'stereotyped diamond-studded
syrens' on the one hand and for Henry's kneejerk
assumption of the role of betrayed husband on the other.

This undermining of sexual stereotypes closely
resembles the style of some notable Hollywood comedies
of the thirties and forties – for instance those starring
Katharine Hepburn and Spencer Tracy, or the Howard
Hawks movies which partnered Cary Grant with a variety
of leading ladies. They presented forcible and independent
women and often showed conventional masculinist
assumptions meeting a sticky end. Grant in particular was
shown in a variety of undignified situations: while the

camera never denied his physical charm, as legendary as Coward's, his stuffy male persona was subjected to severe shocks; he fell into rivers, chased leopards, dressed in womens' clothes – and invariably, by the end of the film, admitted to liking it. As Andrew Britton puts it, he learned

> To identify 'play', in the sense of recovered infantile polymorphousness . . . with 'sophistication', the apogee of cultivated adulthood. The sophisticated couple is the couple whose sexuality is no longer identified by the phallus. The characteristic co-presence in these works of the two apparently distinct modes of farce and wit is the expression of this thematic principle. The partners engage in rough-house and in epigram and repartee; the anarchic consorts with the urbane; the infantile drives which precede maturity and civilisation are suddenly definitive of them.[22]

The mixture of 'rough-house and epigram', the playfulness, are qualities equally necessary in the performing of Coward, and the style of acting embraced by these comedies, authoritative, forthright and lively, is one which productions of his work might do well to emulate. There is, however, a certain difference in the underlying attitudes of the Hawks films and Coward's plays. The 'playful couples' of the films were invariably married off at the end: the implication seems to be that there is a place for 'play' in helping both men and women to grow, but that when playtime is over they have to become responsible members of the existing social order. Coward's characters remain free to go on playing; but they also remain outside the social order to some extent; they do not marry, or if they do, it is not necessarily the end of the story; and while they may be freer of the conventional assumptions about sexuality that afflict the characters at the beginning of a Hawks movie, that freedom carries its own pain and confusion with it; the bitter edge to the laughter at the end of *Design for Living* reflects this.

Both the playful attitude to stereotypes and the awareness of relationships as volatile and transient have their effect on the style of the love scenes. In most plays, the presence of a pair of lovers tends to demand that we identify with them but also remain in a slightly voyeuristic relationship to them; their love is essentially a private matter which we are privileged to watch. With Coward's lovescenes, however, we are clearly invited spectators watching a conscious performance; the characters express not only desire for each other but also an ironic awareness that they are playing a role – a role which affords them, and us, pleasure. When they play against the lines, they are fully aware that they are joining in a game; their performer's charm ensures that it is played well:

GARRY *PROWLING ABOUT*: How was the Toscanini concert?

JOANNA: Glorious. (*SHE SITS DOWN*) He played the Eighth and the Seventh.

GARRY: Personally I prefer the Fifth.

JOANNA: I like the Ninth best of all.

GARRY *CASUALLY SITTING BESIDE HER ON THE SOFA*: There's nothing like the dear old Ninth.

JOANNA: I love the Queen's Hall, don't you? It's so uncompromising.

GARRY *TAKING HER HAND*: I love the Albert Hall much more.

JOANNA *LEANING AGAINST HIM*: I wonder why. I aways find it depressing.

GARRY: *TAKING HER IN HIS ARMS*: Not when they're
  doing 'Hiawatha', surely?
JOANNA *DREAMILY*: Even then.
GARRY *HIS MOUTH ON HERS*: I won't hear a word
  against the Albert Hall.

This works, not by presenting us with a conventionally
erotic love scene, but by drawing us into an in-joke; the
energy of these two performers draws us into a game. We
help them endow these idiotic words with an erotic charge.
In doing so we celebrate the frivolity that makes this
possible; we enjoy the way that frivolity transcends
conventional sex-roles; the lovers here are androgynous
partners in the game rather than the female 'hunter' and
the male 'prey' which they appear to be at the beginning of
the scene, when Joanna arrives in full warpaint and
produces her story about a lost latch-key. It is an effect
common in Coward's love-scenes; the performer's instinct
shared by most of his central characters charms us into
seeing desire in an unfamiliar, ironic light, but one which in
no way diminishes its powerful onstage magic. This process
of continually drawing us into a game, continually dwelling
on passion but distancing us from it, is perhaps best
summed up by Barthes's word *erotisation* – a process of
energising and enlivening; for these scenes invariably
increase the pace of the play and challenge conventional
assumptions about sexuality.

It is not the erotic but erotisation which is a positive
value. Erotisation is a product of the erotic: light,
diffusive, mercurial; which circulates without
coagulating; a multiple and mobile flirtation links the
subject to what passes, pretends to cling, then lets go for
something else (and then, sometimes, this variable

landscape is severed, sliced through by a sudden
immobility: love).[23]

To control the erotic mood of a play in this way takes not
merely a playwright's instinct but an actor's; Coward drew
throughout his career on his own stage presence. In looking
more closely at his major comedies I hope to show in more
detail the use he made of it.

6
Five Comedies

I am no good at love
My heart should be wise and free
I kill the unfortunate golden goose
Whoever it may be
With over-articulate tenderness
And too much intensity.[1]

I. 'No good at love': *Private Lives* and *Design for Living*

Two people are close; they try to pass the time, get bored,
quarrel, crack jokes; they encounter two other people and
don't make much of them; nothing really happens; at the
end of the play they are in the same state as they were at the
beginning. If this sounds like *Waiting for Godot* this is not
wholly coincidental. For all his dislike of the style and form
employed by the Theatre of the Absurd, Coward
dramatised in the story of Elyot and Amanda the sense of
inhabiting a universe without meaning or controlling force;
in the twenties, anticipating Beckett, he earned a label for

himself in Robert Graves's summary of that decade: 'Coward was the dramatist of disillusion, as Eliot was its tragic poet, Aldous Huxley its novelist, and James Joyce its prose epic-writer.'[2]

The difference between Coward and this exalted company is not so much one of attitude as one of resonance. Beckett, or the Eliot of *The Waste Land*, or Joyce, convey with irresistible force the sense of possibilities exhausted, of convictions tested on the intellect and the nerves and found wanting; the bare conditions of the *Godot* tramps reflect their existential stripping, the one slim conviction on which they ground themselves. Coward's characters, stripped of beliefs, have egos to keep them going; they forget the outside world to live luxuriously like exotic waterflies on a surface tension composed of personal charm and the admiration it attracts. If they have a conviction amid their foggy awareness of 'cosmic thingummies', it's a belief in love: not love as a redeeming factor in existence, a goal to strive for, but as a mischievous presence that will creep up on you somehow and strip you of charm and dignity; despite all evidence to the contrary, they cannot help thinking that, this time, things might be different, that they will manage not to kill the golden goose even though they have no intention of changing themselves.

Rebecca West wrote an epitaph on Coward, a lifelong friend, that is all the more touching for its ruthless honesty:

> A sensitive man, he was also a vain man. He talked constantly about himself, thought about himself, catalogued his achievements, evaluated them, presented to listeners such conclusions as were favourable, and expected, and waited for, applause.
>
> His sensitivity knew this and was shocked, and he

regularly rough-housed his own vanity by considering himself in a ridiculous light. This he did for the good of his soul. The public image of himself in top-hat and tails, the immortal spirit of the charming twenties, was merely one of his admirable inventions. It was a disguise worn by an odd and selective kind of Puritan.[3]

This 'rough-housing' is the source of comic energy in *Private Lives*; Coward dramatises the relationship between the performer's vanity and vulnerability, allowing full rein to his own onstage charisma, and that of Lawrence, but never allowing himself, or the audience, to take it wholly seriously. Both Elyot and Amanda are accomplished mask-makers; this makes them dangerously attractive, and they duly act as honeypots to their new and uninspiring spouses. But to be loved for the sake of the mask is not satisfying to the wearer, who then becomes trapped behind it. When we first meet Amanda and Victor, it is clear that he has been captivated by her in a role she is now sick of playing, that of little girl lost:

VICTOR: I don't believe you're nearly as complex as you think you are.

AMANDA: I don't think I'm particularly complex, but I know I'm unreliable.

VICTOR: You're frightening me horribly. In what way unreliable?

AMANDA: I'm so apt to see things the wrong way round.

VICTOR: What sort of things?

AMANDA: Morals. What one should do and what one shouldn't.

VICTOR *FONDLY*: Darling, you're so sweet.

AMANDA: Thank you, Victor, that's most encouraging.

149

The alternative, of course, is to be seen through the mask. When Elyot and Amanda meet on the balcony after five years of divorce, it is this ability to see through each other that re-creates the attraction between them; they slice through the persiflage about sacred elephants to admit clearly that the love is still there. 'You don't hold any mystery for me darling, do you mind?' says Elyot. 'There isn't a particle of you that I don't know, remember, and want.'

But once they are together, this same ability to see through the mask becomes less alluring. While they can gaily puncture the preconceptions of Sybil and Victor about sex-roles, they can't maintain the same carefree attitudes towards each other:

> AMANDA: When we were together, did you really think I was unfaithful to you?
> ELYOT: Yes, practically every day.
> AMANDA: I thought you were too; often I used to torture myself with visions of your bouncing about on divans with awful widows.

It is a critical cliché that their position is tragic: unhappy together, unhappy apart. But the reason for that position, grounded in egotism, is comic. Beckett's *Film* once showed a man in flight from the fact of being perceived, even by a dog or cat; Elyot and Amanda can't bear *not* to be seen; why else the Molyneux dress, the carefully cultivated act at the piano? But at the same time they are deeply ambivalent about being seen *through*. They want to be simultaneously understood and retain the 'mystery' that Amanda jeers at. She sends up the idea of mask-making as a coy 'feminine' preoccupation, wielding her lipstick satirically in front of Elyot, but, at the same time, she wants to retain a certain distance. She wants to be adored but also to puncture the adoring pose of the lover if she chooses:

> ELYOT *BURYING HIS FACE IN HER SHOULDER*: I do love you so.
> AMANDA: Don't blow, dear heart, it gives me the shivers.

Elyot feels threatened by Sybil's promise to 'understand' him; his description of their relationship as 'something tremendously cosy' has a slight satirical edge; clearly he feels that she is not really equal to 'understanding' him and shows, already, a mild contempt for her; 'completely feminine little creature' is a just but not a loving epithet. On the other hand, Amanda's ability to puncture his romantic self-image with 'It's too soon after dinner' sends him into frenzies of ill-temper. Both of them despise people who take them at face value and dislike those who don't.

Private Lives never stops to analyse this paradox; it dramatises every facet of it with a quicksilver liveliness which springs from Coward's application of his craft to the abilities of his original cast. The *rapport* between Coward and Gertrude Lawrence was legendary; T. E. Lawrence, who himself understood the workings of a carefully created persona, attended a rehearsal which, as he later wrote to Coward, gave him greater pleasure than the finished production because 'I could not always tell when you were acting and when talking to one another.'[4] Gertrude Lawrence was as accomplished a mask maker as Coward. He wrote of her:

> Gertie has an astounding sense of the complete reality of the moment, and her moments, dictated by the extreme variability of her moods, change so swiftly that it is frequently difficult to discover what, apart from eating, sleeping and acting, is true of her at all.[5]

Her personality informs the role of Amanda as Coward's did that of Elyot. 'It was all there,' he recalled after the first night, 'the witty, quicksilver delivery of the lines; the romantic quality, tender and alluring; the swift, brittle rages.'[6]

But the play is more than a couple of life studies or a convenient context for the magic of a particular *rapport*. It is also, as Coward pointed out, a technically demanding work, exploiting not only the personalities of the original cast but their special expertise. Both had distinguished themselves in revue; in fact Amanda was Lawrence's first dramatic role. Coward impacted revue techniques onto a full-length plot; he demanded the rapid changes in mood and pace he and Lawrence demonstrated in *London Calling!*, the same transitions from speech to song or dance, the same ability to throw away a vinegary *non-sequitur* like 'Very flat, Norfolk' with a deftness that places it as a laugh line while allowing the action to go on; and through the technical fireworks explores the emotional implications of the performer's chameleon charm. The play consists of a series of scenes which bear a close resemblance to revue sketches: newly married couples exchange awkward pleasantries at the start of the honeymoon (Coward himself wrote a sketch about wedding nights through the ages, from Victorian timidity to twenties cynicism); two lovers begin with sweet nothings and end in furious battle; two couples who have swapped partners have an excruciatingly embarrassing breakfast together; a pair of respectable strangers come to blows. Cutting across these individual episodes is the ebb and flow of the relationship between Elyot and Amanda, sometimes powerful enough to bring all action to a standstill as they contemplate their latest failure to co-exist in peace.

Superimposed over the sketches too is a very precise

structure which anchors the apparently plotless story and also allows us simultaneously to admire the protagonists' energy and style and to laugh at their egotism. Bergson maintained that comedy in its most basic, slapstick form depended on the sight of a human being temporarily made to resemble a machine; the man who slips on the banana skin is suddenly reduced to a mechanical toy, controlled by something outside himself. *Private Lives* turns its characters into a very sophisticated toy indeed. Their feelings may be 'big romantic stuff' but circumstances force them into a pattern whose symmetry works against love's spontaneity. Act One opens with Sybil and Elyot on their balcony, discussing his first wife; there follows a scene with Amanda and Victor, who do exactly the same thing. Elyot and Amanda meet, and the result is two identical scenes in which they try to persuade their respective partners to leave for Paris. Both scenes end in quarrels which leave Elyot and Amanda alone on their balconies, not only in the same place for the same reason, but even carrying identical props, a pair of champagne cocktails apiece.

This ruthless symmetry is made more comic in contrast to the self-assurance of the protagonists and their apparent wealth which seems, at first, to give them total control over their own destinies. Coward's original production made use of his own talent for music; the second act, with the runaway pair alone in Paris, saw him improvising on the piano to gloss over a developing quarrel. To some of his critics this suggested padding, but it also underlined Elyot's poise. Of Lawrence as Amanda, the choreographer Agnes de Mille wrote, 'When she walks, she streams, when she kicks, she flashes. Her speaking voice is a kind of song, quite unrealistic but lovely.'[7] In other words, Elyot and Amanda are both self-created works of art, and the relentless coincidences to which the play subjects them are an elegant equivalent of the custard pie in the face. The symmetry was stressed alongside the elegance: popping in and out onto the balconies like dolls in an Art Deco weather-house, characters frequently found themselves duplicating not just situations but even gestures; Coward and Lawrence perched on the rails in identical positions, legs crossed, arms similarly draped; they might have eyed each other belligerently but the unconscious harmony of their body-language not only made them look ridiculous but also suggested that, subconsciously, they were still close. As they stared out front, hands forming a pattern along the rails, expressions equally disgruntled, they resorted to a mixture of insult and small talk:

AMANDA: Whose yacht is that?
ELYOT: The Duke of Westminster's I expect. It always is.
AMANDA: I wish I were on it.
ELYOT: I wish you were on it too.

Adrienne Allen and Laurence Olivier fell into identical poses at the end of the first act; as the curtain fell they were uttering virtually identical lines like some idiotically irrelevant chorus. The overall effect is of a ludicrous mechanism which, time after time, knocks the carefully constructed mask of charm for six and leaves the egos of the charming face to face, naked and resentful, 'no good at love' because they are incapable of self-abandon, but too fond of attention to try and do without it.

If charm cannot preserve harmony between the charming, however, it can still provide a defence against the outside world. Elyot and Amanda may fight like panthers when they are alone together, but they also realise that they are 'figures of fun all right', and their sense of style offers a way of dealing gracefully with the situation they

have irresponsibly created. Only days after their escape
from Sybil and Victor they have to face them; arriving with
righteous triumph in the middle of a ferocious fight
between Elyot and Amanda, the cast-off spouses provide a
comic version of Banquo's ghost, reproach incarnate; the
response of their erring partners is to summon their play
instinct to ease the tension:

SYBIL: It's all perfectly horrible. I feel smirched and
    unclean as though slimy things had been crawling all
    over me.
ELYOT: Maybe they have, that's a very old sofa.
VICTOR: If you don't stop your damned flippancy, I'll
    knock your head off.
ELYOT: Has it ever struck you that flippancy might cover a
    very real embarrassment?

Sybil and Victor may have morality on their side, but Elyot
and Amanda have manners on theirs; Victor's Puritanical
insistence on creating discomfort for its own sake serves to
assert the primacy of charm over rectitude; as Coward once
again plays symmetrical games, pairing up Elyot and Victor
and Amanda and Sybil for the next quarrel, it becomes
more and more apparent that Elyot and Amanda are
inevitably going to be forced into an alliance against their
spouses' self-satisfaction. Typically, it forms over a trivial
incident. Coward brings the two couples together for a
quiet interlude for the first time; and in the discomfort of
breakfast and all its forced intimacy a silly joke is enough to
start things off; Amanda fills in an awkward silence with a
stream of persiflage about travel, 'arriving at strange
places, and seeing strange people, and eating strange
foods':

155

ELYOT: And making strange noises afterwards.

AMANDA CHOKES VIOLENTLY, VICTOR JUMPS UP AND TRIES TO OFFER ASSISTANCE, BUT SHE WAVES HIM AWAY AND CONTINUES TO CHOKE.

VICTOR *TO ELYOT*: That was a damned fool thing to do.

ELYOT: How did I know she was going to choke?

VICTOR *TO AMANDA*: Here, drink some coffee.

AMANDA *BREATHLESSLY GASPING*: Leave me alone. I'll be all right in a minute.

VICTOR *TO ELYOT*: You waste too much time trying to be funny.

In one last movement of his symmetrical machine, Coward sets off Victor and Sybil arguing about whether Elyot's remark was funny or not; as the strain of their enforced togetherness over the last few days finally begins to tell, they shift to personal abuse and then into violence, repeating the scene between Elyot and Amanda which they interrupted at the end of the second act. Over their screams and shouts, Elyot and Amanda wordlessly renew the bond between them; they know what they find funny and they also know that this is important, and the knowledge leads them to tiptoe away from the chaos they have caused in perfect amity. It is clearly a temporary amity; but, Coward implies, their frivolity offers them at least a chance of coping with the indignities of love.

It is not the least of Coward's achievements in the play that he convinces us, momentarily, that this *is* a happy ending. Desmond MacCarthy remarked that 'he has . . . disguised the grimness of his play . . . his conception of love is really desolating.'[8] But for some of its early critics, this very deftness betrayed the play into trivialising the issues it raised; Ivor Brown, for instance, paid tribute to the sparkle of the evening's entertainment but predicted that 'Within a few years the student of drama will be sitting in complete bewilderment . . . wondering what on earth those fellows in 1930 saw in so flimsy a trifle.'[9] The play remains a repertory staple; the reason, perhaps, is that the bravura of Elyot's attack on seriousness and the 'poor philosophers' continues to disarm; it is, after all, the business of frivolity to dodge awkward questions, and they are rarely dodged with more style than here. Coward, however, continued to explore the relationship between love and charm, between emotion and mask. In *Design For Living*, produced on Broadway only three years after the London opening of *Private Lives*, he took more risks; the result was a disappointingly short run (135 nights) and objections from the Lord Chamberlain which prevented it from opening in London until 1939.

It remains a curiously underrated play. Coward wrote of it in *Play Parade One*:

> It has been liked and disliked, and hated and admired, but never, I think, sufficiently loved by any but its three leading actors. This, perhaps, was only to be expected, as its central theme . . . must appear to be definitely anti-social. People were certainly interested and entertained and occasionally even moved by it, but it seemed, to many of them, 'unpleasant'.[10]

The difficulty lies, perhaps, not so much in that central theme itself as from a failure to read correctly the way it is treated. The story is about two men and a woman who all love one another and who exchange partners within the group several times before apparently settling down together. In 1933 this was considered 'shocking' or 'unpleasant'. When the play opened in London in 1939, with war already on the horizon, the critical response was a weary tolerance for its 'smartly silly'[11] attempt to be sensational; the *Observer* summed it up briskly as 'a hangover from the twittering twenties'.[12] John Lahr, in 1982, largely shares this view; he sees the plot as 'belaboured sensationalism' and complains that the 'issue (*sic*) of abnormal sexuality and success are never fully integrated into the action of the play'.[13] His summary of the play's ending – 'The homosexual daydream of sexual abundance comes true'[14] seems to confirm that he sees the 'issue' discussed by the play as one of sexual orientation. This, I think, is the misreading of Coward's focus in *Design for Living* that has dogged it from the outset. The relationship between Leo and Otto is not the focal point of the play; still less does Coward impose upon it value-judgements like 'normal' or 'abnormal', or implicitly advocate what Ernest, the voice of orthodoxy in the play, calls 'this disgusting three-sided erotic hotch-potch' as a 'design for living' for anyone but the three protagonists. He is, rather, concerned with the interplay between the public and the private face; the private face here consists of affections and emotions and also of creative ability: Otto is a painter, Leo a writer, and Gilda an interior designer who also acts as critic and gadfly to both the men. The public face is the way these affections and talents operate in the world; all three protagonists achieve some success in their chosen *métiers* and have to evolve a relationship to their public; they also have to integrate this relationship into their personal lives; all three, too, are attractive and aware of it; this fact sometimes cuts across their affection, their mutual loyalty and also the partnerships they form at different stages in the play; it can lead them into playing conventionalised sex-roles, into manipulativeness and into jealousy.

The private faces of Leo, Otto and Gilda are thus bound up with their professional lives; talent and charm are attributes which they can market; this, in turn, means that they are also capable of standing back from their masks in a way that Elyot and Amanda, performers by instinct, cannot; within *Design for Living* there are fewer violent emotional transitions from tenderness to rage, charm to malice; instead charm is ruthlessly analysed – and we then see characters struggling to cope emotionally with what they have already understood intellectually.

The change reflects the talents of Coward's chosen cast for the play. *Design for Living* was a project conceived and written for Coward himself and his close friends Alfred Lunt and Lynn Fontanne; as he wrote in *Present Indicative*, it was a project predicated upon the eventual acquisition, by all three of them, of successful public faces – the persona of a star:

> From these shabby, uncongenial rooms we projected ourselves into future eminence. We discussed, the three of us, over potato salad and dill pickles, our most secret dreams of success. Lynn and Alfred were to be married. That was the first plan. Then they were to become definitely idols of the public. That was the second plan. Then, all this being successfully accomplished, they were to act exclusively together. This was the third plan. It remained for me to supply the fourth, which was than when all three of us had become stars of sufficient magnitude to be able to count upon an individual following irrespective of each other, then, poised serenely upon that enviable plane of achievement, we would meet and act triumphantly together . . .[15]

If this long-standing friendship founded on shared ambition made the play's subject – success and the public face – inevitable, the special qualities of the Lunts had a profound effect upon its style. The three of them had an onstage *rapport* as powerful as that of Coward and Lawrence – Coward and Alfred Lunt once inadvertently swapped lines for almost a whole scene and found it no great strain to carry on; but the talents of Lunt and Fontanne were very different from those of Lawrence. While she worked on instinct, their approach to acting was to treat it as a series of problems to be solved by intelligence and painstaking rehearsal. Lunt spent hours working out exactly the right way to close a door. No detail was too small. Fontanne made changes throughout the run of the play; only on the last night did she manage to develop a mechanism to create the sort of handbag that fitted Gilda's character – a small spring caused a mass of clutter to boil over like a pan of milk whenever it was opened. Highly respected stars, they worked for a long time with the Theatre Guild whose policy of high quality plays on a low budget they admired, and encouraged writers to experiment with challenging themes. *Design for Living* marked their return to Broadway.

About five years previously Lynne Fontanne had appeared as Nina Leeds in O'Neill's *Strange Interlude*, the longest role yet written for an actress. Nina is torn between two men, a situation O'Neill explores in tragic depth for more than five hours; it prompted Groucho Marx in *Animal Crackers* to leer to a pair of starlets 'We three would make an ideal couple. Pardon me while I have a strange interlude.' Coward's attitude to the play was no more reverent; Fontanne asked for his advice on the part and at her instigation he sat twice through what he described as 'the whole bloody nine acts of that bore'.[16] In fact, however, the play seems to have made some impact on him for many of the issues it raises are also examined in

Design for Living. In both plays the woman is the emotional and intellectual centre, and in both plays she is unable to function in a conventional marriage. Both, too, demand frequent transitions from action to introspection and analysis. In *Strange Interlude* the characters speak their thoughts aloud for our benefit; Coward, less experimentally, allows his trio to confide in one another or in Ernest, their friend and butt.

But if Coward's technique is more conventional, the way in which he explores the issues raised by the triangular situation is less so; although *Design for Living* is styled 'a comedy' it does not trivialise the questions examined by O'Neill but looks at them from a different angle.

Strange Interlude opens at a point where Nina has lost the man she really loves; she passionately regrets that they did not sleep together before his death and it soon becomes clear that neither of the two men who love her is an adequate substitute. She marries Sam, who becomes obsessed with making money, but learns that there is a streak of madness in his family and turns to Ned, her other lover, to give her a child. All three are plunged into a torment of jealousy which destroys them completely: Sam's greed reaches lunatic proportions, Ned slumps into promiscuity and allows Nina to treat him like a slave, and Nina herself becomes a jealous, even a cruel, mother. She tries to discover some system of beliefs on which to act and can only reiterate the conclusions of Sam's mother: 'Being happy, that's the nearest we can ever come to knowing what's good!'[17]

The unspoken assumption of the play is that jealousy is part and parcel of sexuality; once aroused it cannot be checked and will rage until it has destroyed everything around it like a forest fire; its seeds are planted even before Nina takes Ned as her lover; she is eternally making comparisons between Ned and Sam and her dead Gordon. This destructiveness is the dark side of love, which, O'Neill implies, is also an irresistible emotion, a passion which cannot be explained or resisted.

For Coward in *Design for Living*, both love and jealousy are problems to be faced and analysed; although he does not pretend to offer solutions he implies that it is, at least sometimes, possible for the characters who experience them to transcend them in shared understanding and perhaps laughter. Sexual attractiveness is not an uncontrollable force but part of charm's armoury, which can be used at will: both Leo and Gilda, guilty after their amorous encounter, feel that they have been playing the roles of sexual stereotype. 'There are moments in life when I look upon my own damned femininity with complete nausea', says Gilda:

> It humiliates me to the dust to think that I can go so far, clearly and intelligently, keeping faith with my own standards – which are not female standards at all – preserving a certain decent integrity, not using any tricks; then suddenly, something happens, a spark is struck and down I go into the mud! Squirming with archness, being aloof and desirable, consciously alluring, snatching and grabbing, evading and surrendering, dressed and painted for victory.

Leo similarly describes himself as 'like a mannequin. New spring model, with a few extra flounces.'

The 'extra flounces' consist of artistic success; Leo has, he admits, been showing off to Gilda, buying champagne with the takings from his latest play. 'There seemed to be something new about you', says Gilda. 'Perhaps it's having money.' Otto, when they admit that they spent the night together, also sees sexual attraction and success as intertwined. When they try to persuade him to think calmly, he rounds on Gilda with 'I expect your reason and intelligence prompted you to wear your green dress, didn't it? With the emerald earrings? And your green shoes, too, although they hurt you when you dance', and walks out after making it clear to Leo that his jealousy has more than one facet. 'Go ahead, my boy, and do great things! You've already achieved a Hotel de Luxe, a few smart suits and the woman I loved.'

As the second act begins, Coward shows the two sides of Leo's charm, success and attractiveness, pulling against each other. Gilda refuses to delude herself about the quality of his work and resents his preoccupation with what she calls 'second-hand people' who lionize him. Barbs are visible through the banter:

LEO *READING THE* DAILY MIRROR: *'Change and Decay* is gripping throughout. The characterisation falters here and there, but the dialogue is polished and sustains a high level from first to last and is frequently witty, nay, even brilliant –
GILDA: I love 'nay'.
LEO: But – here we go, dear! But the play, on the whole, is decidedly thin.
GILDA: My God! They've noticed it.
LEO: *JUMPING UP*: Thin – thin! What do they mean, 'Thin'?
GILDA: Just thin, darling. Thin's thin all over the world and you can't get away from it.
LEO: Would you call it thin?
GILDA: Emaciated.

When Otto turns up, also, now, a great success, it is

inevitable that Gilda will fall into his arms, but the scene is not a mere re-run of the previous episode with Leo. They debate the ethics of the situation as before, they create a halo of glamour around the moment – 'a moment to remember, all right,' says Otto. 'Scribble it on your heart; a flicker of ecstasy sandwiched between yesterday and tomorrow – something to be recaptured in the future without illusion, perfect in itself!' But the moment takes place nonetheless in a resolutely prosaic setting which constantly undermines it; they assemble a scratch meal of oddments rather than the glamorous trappings of Leo's night with Gilda and punctuate reflections on the nature of love with suggestions about the best sort of jam to eat with the rice pudding. Gilda realises that one element of the love she felt for both men has vanished: they do not need her any more. Otto sums up their old relationship succinctly:

> Leo and I were both struggling, a single line was in both our minds leading to success – that's what we were planning for, working like dogs for! You helped us both, jostling us on to the line again when we slipped off and warming us when we were cold in discouragement.

He rightly points out that the old days cannot be brought back but he also fails to offer more than a brief flare of desire as a new ground base for love; now that the struggles are over, what place is there for Gilda? Her own solution is to walk out on the pair of them, determined to be herself for the first time, to learn 'the lesson of paddling my own canoe . . . not just weighing down somebody else's and imagining I'm steering it.'

The plot has already begun to move with the comic symmetry of *Private Lives*. Coward now turns it into a pattern so relentlessly symmetrical that it becomes a lunatic ritual. The last possible permutation of the three lovers, Leo and Otto, open the notes that Gilda has left – identical in content, propped against the brandy-bottle like a pair of bookends – get drunk and fall weepily into each other's arms. As they work their way down the brandy bottle they recapitulate all the arguments of the play – about passion, about success, about need; as they get drunker and drunker the effect is like a record played at the wrong speed, fast and garbled and then grinding to a slurred and grating stop. They arrive at three decisions, all vaguely imcompatible: they will sell themselves as hard as they can for 'More and better Success! Louder and funnier Success!' They will get away from the corruption of civilisation:

> OTTO: You'd soon be all right if you got away from all this muck.
> LEO: Yes, I know, but how?
> OTTO: *PUTTING HIS ARM ROUND HIS SHOULDER*: Get on a ship, Leo – never mind where it's going! Just get on a ship – a small ship.
> LEO: How small?
> OTTO: Very small indeed; a freighter.
> LEO: Is that what you did?
> OTTO: Yes.
> LEO: Then I will. Where do very small ships sail from?

And they are, without Gilda, going to be 'awfully – awfully – lonely.'

Their alliance explodes the conventional posture of jealous lover which they both found necessary to adopt previously; now that jealousy has flown out of the window they are free to win Gilda back, and, in the final act, this is what they do. Gilda has also achieved success by selling herself: married to the conventional Ernest, she lives in a luxurious flat full of paintings and antiques – all of them for sale; she refers to it as 'my shop' and appears to be doing well. Throughout the play the sets and costumes have grown more and more expensive; Gladys Calthrop's design for the last act was almost aggressively fashionable and had a flavour of the luxury liner about it. All three have sold out their talent; the results are charming but, in the end, they have all behaved like Gilda in her green dress, making themselves attractive without a thought for integrity. But the fact that they are all three equally successful banishes the question of 'need' from their relationship. All that remains is for the tight little group anarchically to define itself against the conventional world. Otto and Leo arrive while Gilda is entertaining some rich and pompous guests; they proceed to drive them away by undermining all their small talk with devastating rudeness:

> HELEN: It's funny how people alter; only the other day in the Colony a boy that I used to know when he was at Yale walked up to my table, and I didn't recognise him!
>
> LEO: Just fancy!
>
> OTTO: Do you know, I have an excellent memory for names, but I cannot for the life of me remember faces. Sometimes I look at Leo suddenly and haven't the faintest idea who he is.

They stay on, popping up to greet Ernest the next morning in borrowed pyjamas like a pair of antic jack-in-the-boxes and treating him with brisk patronage as a 'dear old pet'; Gilda is finally and ineluctably drawn into the game, recognising that she is 'not different from them. We're all of a piece, the three of us'. As Ernest walks out they are united in howls of laughter – and, in Coward's first production, physically entwined in a complicated three-cornered knot, a circle impossible to break from inside or outside.

Several questions, of course, remain unanswered. In the drunk scene Coward allows the boozy expansiveness of Otto and Leo to raise some apparently incompatible ideas about commercial success and artistic integrity, and having jammed them side by side for a laugh he never re-examines them in the light of sober day. It was, indeed, a question Coward never quite answered to his own satisfaction. There remains, too, the question of whether talent and mutual attraction can hold the three together – Gilda, after all, left the group for reasons concerned precisely with that question of success. Nor have we ever seen them operating as a group of three, but always as a pair with one outsider – Otto or Leo, feeling themselves betrayed in turn, Gilda confiding to Ernest that she is leaving.

But although this is never discussed, there are visual signals that guide the audience towards acceptance of the conclusion as inevitable. As we have seen, characters find themselves moving in symmetrical patterns, like the quartet in *Private Lives*; but here the patterns are accepted and, in the case of this last tableau, chosen; the trio choose to resign themselves to the indignities love forces upon them and to create a way of life that allows for them.

After the London opening, *The Times* claimed to detect two strains at work; 'Sometimes . . . a serious play and a deeply interesting. Sometimes . . . Mr. Coward's dialogue dips and swings and glitters as though he were writing farce.'[18] The two modes, however, are united in these accepted patterns. Farce forces its characters into similar situations; frequently they become mechanical toys geared entirely to hiding in cupboards and under beds. *Design for Living* reverses this activity. The characteristic movements

of Leo and Otto are not those of concealment but of
self-disclosure; Gilda may hide them from Ernest with
ludicrous stories ('He's had the most awful neuralgia . . .
his little face is all pinched and strained') but among the
three of them everything is admitted, albeit reluctantly.
However callously they behave to Ernest and the rest of the
world, however outrageously they strike poses, their
fundamental honesty within the group gives the play
moments of unusual tenderness. A production by Michael
Blakemore in 1973 stressed this; the sets and costumes
underlined the tendency of the three to play roles: Vanessa
Redgrave as Gilda spent her time in the Paris flat in an
assortment of unbecoming ethnic garments and Jeremy
Brett as the departing Otto affected a shabby but dashing
hat and a worker's kitbag that suggested the radical chic of
the Auden generation. At the same time, their stance when
together was upright and frank and their eyes met as they
struggled to account for their amorous comings and goings.
For Sheridan Morley, Coward's friend and biographer, the
production illustrated admirably the characteristic Coward
attitude to love and talent: 'Live with your success, put up
with its inconveniences, revel in its joys, never complain,
never explain.'[19]

II. *'Improbable Farce': Blithe Spirit.*

Had a few drinks, then went to Savoy. Pretty bad blitz
. . . a couple of bombs fell very near during dinner. Wall
bulged a bit and door flew in. Orchestra went on playing
. . . I sang . . . On the whole a very strange and amusing
evening.[20]

Coward spend much of his war abroad, but in the first half
of 1941 he set up the project that was to become *In Which*

We Serve, wrote *Blithe Spirit* in five days and opened it within six weeks. It was to have one of the longest recorded runs in the British theatre.

If the shape of *Private Lives* looks forward to *Waiting for Godot*, *Blithe Spirit* could be seen as a forerunner of Beckett's *Play*, which shows three characters, all dead, endlessly repeating the story of their triangular relationship. The comparison is, of course, ludicrous; nothing could be further from the tone of *Play* than the anarchic flippancy of *Blithe Spirit*; but, given that Coward's play originated and entertained London in the bloodiest period of its history, it is worth noting the fact; the time and the subject matter would appear to dictate an approach closer to Beckett's.

The twenties and thirties had seen an upsurge of interest in the paranormal, in clairvoyance and spiritualism, and it was reflected in the theatre. Plays like Barrie's *Mary Rose* or Priestley's *Johnson over Jordan* provided a society that was rapidly losing its religious faith with a reassurance that death was not the end. Gareth Lloyd Evans sees in the popularity of the plays a hunger for confirmation that the sacrifices of the First World War had not been in vain, 'a passionate faith that loved ones who, in reality, had been blown to pieces in the trenches had passed on to a bourne from which they could not return but which was a place of happiness and content.'[21] Coward explodes these gentle assumptions: in *Blithe Spirit* the dead do not exist to make the lives of the living more comfortable. On the other hand, he also parodies the newer attitudes to the dead found in popular works of the late thirties and forties: one of the biggest box-office successes in the cinema in 1940 was Hitchcock's film of Daphne du Maurier's Gothic novel *Rebecca*. Here the mousey heroine has to struggle against the powerful personality of her husband's dead wife;

although there is no suggestion that she has survived the grave in any form, the force of her character is strong enough to destroy the house in which she had lived and threaten the new marriage. Death here is the bringer of anarchy, danger and sexual energy.

This is also true of *Blithe Spirit*. The ordered life of the hero, Charles Condomine, is disrupted when a séance calls up the ghost of his first wife, Elvira; she hangs about the house, bringing chaos in her wake and eventually bringing about the death of his second wife Ruth – whereupon Ruth too materialises in ghostly form and the two spirits bicker over Charles until he finally manages to escape. But while du Maurier virtually equates anarchy with evil, Coward's attitude is more ambivalent: the eventually routing of the ghosts is clearly a 'happy ending', but their energy is something to be celebrated. We may pity Charles, but he is not an attractive character and the presence of Elvira is a fitting punishment for his self-satisfied and exploitative behaviour: as the play opens he is discussing his first marriage with Ruth:

RUTH: Does it still hurt – when you think of her?
CHARLES: No, not really – sometimes I almost wish it did – I feel rather guilty . . .

He is also planning his next book; they are expecting the medium, Madame Arcati, to dinner, so that Charles can study and use her; this appears to be his usual technique:

CHARLES: Do you remember how I got the idea for *The Light Goes Out?*
RUTH *SUDDENLY SEEING THAT HAGGARD, RADDLED WOMAN IN THE HOTEL AT*

> *BIARRITZ*: Of course I remember – we sat up half the
> night talking about it . . .
> CHARLES: She certainly came in very handy – I wonder
> who she was.

The new novel, *The Unseen*, is to be a monument to
scepticism. Charles, in fact, is dodging two vital issues in his
life – passion and personal experience; he has retreated
behind a mask of smoothness, into a relationship based on
'calm', and success based on shrewd analysis of other
peoples' lives. Appropriately he gets his come-uppance at
the hands of two different people – the passionate Elvira
and the innocent Madame Arcati.

In styling the play a 'farce', a term he rarely used,
Coward is allying himself with a tradition which includes
The Comedy of Errors and *The Importance of Being Ernest*
and was to continue with the work of Joe Orton in *What the
Butler Saw* – the tradition of farce as comic existential
nightmare. Coward had little interest in the French farce
tradition of Labiche and Feydeau which is grounded almost
exclusively in the idea of sexual indiscretion in a bourgeois
society: his adaptation for the Royal Court of Feydeau's
Occupe-toi d'Amélie in 1959 contained some splendid jokes
and some flashes of insight into character, but always at the
expense of the manic complexity of the plot. He had still
less interest in the milk-and-water British imitations
grounded in *suspected* sexual indiscretions and involving a
great many lost trousers and episodes in cupboards from
the most innocent motives. In *Blithe Spirit*, it is not Charles's
reputation which is at stake but his sanity. Like Antipholus
of Ephesus and Jack Worthing, he finds that he is not the
person he thought he was: at one point he is threatened
with a psychiatrist and Ruth insists on treating him as 'ill'.

Endangered sanity is of course central to melodrama like

Rebecca, and Coward parodies the idea of the vengeful dead with flippant delight: like Rebecca, Elvira is faithless but possessive; but she also has the inconsequential vagueness of Amanda; she brings the melodrama down to earth by her concern with the small change of passion:

ELVIRA: You never suspected it but I laughed at you steadily from the altar to the grave – all your ridiculous petty jealousies and your fussings and fumings –

CHARLES: You were feckless and irresponsible and morally unstable – I realised that before we left Budleigh Salterton.

ELVIRA: Nobody but a monumental bore would have thought of having a honeymoon at Budleigh Salterton.

CHARLES: What's the matter with Budleigh Salterton?

ELVIRA: I was an eager young bride, Charles – I wanted glamour and music and romance – all I got was potted palms, seven hours a day on a damp golf course and a three-piece orchestra playing 'Merrie England.'

There is a good deal of slapstick fun with flying vases, culminating in the total destruction of the set by the now invisible ghosts of Elvira and Ruth; and the character of Madame Arcati provides a constantly funny refutation of all our pre-conceived ideas about her profession. Neither muttering hag nor Sludge-like charlatan, she radiates innocent enjoyment of life and her work, and this causes her to score off Charles again and again without realising that he is trying to make use of her. She briskly dismisses the clichés of spiritualism – 'I was getting far too sedentary in London, that horrid little flat with the dim lights – they had to be dim, you know, the clients expect it.' Her childlike sensuality, taking pleasure in long bicycle rides, Nature and dry Martinis, links her firmly to the things of this world and makes her work seem ordinary, hardly worth writing novels about; and she has a good line in waspish retorts to sceptical remarks:

RUTH: Daphne is Madame Arcati's control – she's a little girl.

DR BRADMAN: Oh, I see – yes of course.

CHARLES: How old is she?

MADAME ARCATI: Rising seven when she died.

MRS BRADMAN: And when was that?

MADAME ARCATI: February the sixth, 1884.

MRS BRADMAN: Poor little thing.

DR BRADMAN: She must be a bit long in the tooth by now, I should think.

MADAME ARCATI: You should think, Dr Bradman, but I fear you don't – at least, not profoundly enough.

As played by Margaret Rutherford in the original production (Rutherford was chosen by Coward while, oddly enough, playing Mrs Danvers in *Rebecca*) she showed the soul of an intelligent twelve-year old shining through a middle-aged body; dressed in rather childlike garments, such as an Alice band in her hair, she stood for a world of innocence that Charles could not comprehend, let alone exploit; the little maid who proves the unwitting medium through which the ghosts materialise – the bandage she wears round her head a comic version of the Red Indian costume of the cliché 'spirit guide' – adds to the impression of innocence taking its revenge upon scepticism.

But if much of the play is harmlessly comic, it also has a darker dimension. When ghosts appear in folk stories and old ballads they have demands to make, unsatisfied with the present behaviour of those they have left behind. They may call for a cessation of mourning; they may disrupt a newly formed relationship – but they always have to be placated. Keith Thomas writes of the declining belief in ghosts:

> It is now more common for people to live out their full life-span, and to die only after they have retired and withdrawn from an active role in society. This reduces the social vacuum they leave behind. The relative absence of ghosts in modern society can thus be seen as the result of a demographic change – 'the disengaged social situation of the majority of the deceased'. The dead, in other words, fade away before they die. In the earlier periods, by contrast, it was commoner for men to be carried off at the prime of their life, leaving behind them a certain amount of social disturbance, which ghost-beliefs helped to dispel. The period when the soul wandered loose was that when the survivors were adapting themselves to their new pattern of social relationships.[22]

'Social disturbance' in 1941 was, of course, a common feature of the landscape once more; while audiences may not have revived the ghost-beliefs of previous generations they were in a position to understand them and to relish the 'rough-housing' of Charles Condomine's vanity in fancying himself safe behind his mask. He has settled for using his talent in writing second-rate novels and his charm in evading the passion which ought to energise it; he deftly glosses over the anxiety Ruth shows in her assertions about their marriage, assertions which she clearly hopes will be contradicted:

CHARLES: I love you, my love.

RUTH: I know you do – but not the wildest stretch of imagination could describe it as the first fine careless rapture.

CHARLES: Would you like it to be?

RUTH: Good God, no!

CHARLES: Wasn't that a shade too vehement?

RUTH: We're neither of us adolescent, Charles, we've neither of us led exactly prim lives, have we? And we've both been married before – careless rapture at this stage would be incongruous and embarrassing.

CHARLES: I hope I haven't been in any way a disappointment, dear.

Charles is in many ways an early study for Hugo Latymer in his bland asexuality; and although the fact that the passions he is refusing to face were more socially acceptable to the audience of 1941 than Latymer's and hence more acceptable for comic treatment, his 'rough-housing' has its darker moments. Elvira's every entrance is accompanied by a breeze suggestive of the physical passion she represents; her conversation is full of enjoyment of earthly things – flowers, movies, cucumber sandwiches; and she revives in Charles a memory of physical desire:

ELVIRA: That's better.

CHARLES: What's better?

ELVIRA: Your voice was kinder.

CHARLES: Was I ever unkind to you when you were alive?

ELVIRA: Often . . .

CHARLES: Oh, how can you! I'm sure that's an exaggeration.

ELVIRA: Not at all – you were an absolute pig that time we went to Cornwall and stayed in that awful hotel – you hit me with a billiard cue –

175

CHARLES: Only very, very gently . . .
ELVIRA: I loved you very much.
CHARLES: I loved you too. . . .

But at the same time that passion can never find
expression: it is impossible for Charles to touch Elvira and
the fact that it is too late, that she is a ghost, is constantly
stressed by her appearance: Coward calls for her to be
completely grey, skin and clothes and even the things that
she brings with her from beyond the grave, like the grey
roses she carries in the second act. In the first production
Kay Hammond added an unnerving note of sensuality by
adding violently red lipstick to the grey make-up. By the
third act Ruth too is dead and the stage often contains more
grey figures than flesh-coloured ones; at the same time
there is a relentless harping on the subject of physical
passion:

RUTH: You can be as rude as you like, Elvira. I don't mind
a bit – as a matter of fact I should be extremely
surprised if you weren't.
ELVIRA: Why?
RUTH: The reply to that is really too obvious.
CHARLES: I wish you two would stop bickering for one
minute.
RUTH: This is quite definitely one of the most frustrating
nights I have ever spent.
ELVIRA: The reply to that is pretty obvious, too.

There is an edge of real frustration and anger in this
picture, which the Girl-Guide earnestness of Madame
Arcati does not completely dissipate. Similarly, although
Coward reaps a resounding laugh at the end of the second
act when Elivra is attacked by the as yet invisible ghost of
Ruth, the moment at which Ruth's death in announced on

the telephone is not entirely comic: we are also aware of a murderous anger and jealousy towards Charles, whose death Elvira was hoping to achieve by doctoring the car.

Constantly, the play juxtaposes conflicting responses to the situation: we are invited to enjoy the comic lines and the element of parody, but the stage picture, combining the deadly greyness of the ghosts with their often wild physical energy, has a sinister quality. Charles's dilemma, trapped between the old wife and the new, has comic echoes of Elyot Chase, but, unlike Elyot, he is not secure in his own identity: he is accused of being drunk, he imagines that he is having hallucinations, and he cannot ultimately define himself as husband, lover or widower. His final solution, to walk out on the dematerialised spirits and leave them to destroy the house, is done with a fine bravura flourish, but it is the gesture of a man who is not only 'no good at love' but content that this should be so. Charles has, traditionally, been played by actors notable for polish and easy charm – Rex Harrison, Dennis Price, and of course Coward himself; however, a 1976 revival at the National Theatre, directed by Harold Pinter, showed a Charles much more manic and scared at the situation in which he found himself, played by Richard Johnson; and this perhaps recaptured something of the play's ambivalence, its treatment of death as a joke and its simultaneous awareness of the value of life and energy and passion, originally emphasised by its context. A programme note from the first production suggests the spirit in which it was conceived:

> If an air raid warning be received during the performance the audience will be informed from the stage . . . those desiring to leave the theatre may do so but the performance will continue.

III. Comedies of Impingement: *Hay Fever* and *Present Laughter*

'Comedy of impingement' was James Agate's phrase for *The Young Idea* in a review of the 1923 production; in it he also rightly praised Coward as a new and original voice, but it seems strange that he should be the first to devise a label for a kind of comedy which, after all, was certainly not new. The arrival of an exotic stranger or strangers in a conventional community is a common and easily exploited dramatic situation. Subsequently, however, Coward was to reverse this situation to considerable effect. In these two comedies it is the conventional figures who try to impact themselves onto a world where talent rules. The result is a conflict between their conventional values and those which the talented have made for themselves.

In *Hay Fever* the arena for this clash is the country house of the Bliss family. All talented, all totally selfish, they have each invited a guest for the weekend without informing the others. They have thus unwittingly created that seed-bed of Edwardian sexual intrigue, the house-party. Instead of a series of individual encounters they have set up a temporary community; and, as the Edwardians knew, such a community needs to be bound by certain codes of etiquette: relationships may be made and broken, moral taboos preserved or violated, but good manners hold the community together in transient harmony.

The Blisses, however, see manners differently. As the play opens Sorel, who is currently attracted to a diplomat, is flirting with the idea of acquiring some conventional social graces, while Simon asserts the more usual Bliss point of view:

> SOREL: . . . You're right about us being slap-dash, Simon. I wish we weren't.

SIMON: Does it matter?

SOREL: It must, I think – to other people.

SIMON: It's not our fault – it's the way we've been brought up.

SOREL: Well, if we're clever enough to realise that we ought to be clever enough to change ourselves.

SIMON: I'm not sure that I want to.

SOREL: We're so awfully bad-mannered.

SIMON: Not to people we like.

SOREL: The people we like put up with it because they like *us*.

SIMON: What do you mean, exactly, by bad manners? Lack of social tricks and small talk?

Sorel can't answer this adequately, reponding vaguely with 'We've never once asked anyone if they've slept well.' Later, however, when admiring the *savoir-faire* of the diplomat, Richard, she offers a definition which has a slight double edge: 'You always say the right thing, and no one knows a bit what you're really thinking. That's what I adore.'

The Blisses are too ruthless for polite insincerities. David, for instance, has invited his guest, Jackie, to provide material for his next novel; 'she's an abject fool but a useful type', he remarks; under the strain of the unexpected invasion by four guests, he forgets Jackie completely and welcomes her with 'Who the hell are you?' Coward extracts considerable comic mileage out of the guests' attempts to remain polite at all costs. Richard and Jackie, for instance, abandoned in the hall by Simon and Judith who have borne away their own guests without bothering to introduce them, search helplessly to find some common ground:

JACKIE: Have you travelled a lot?

RICHARD *MODESTLY*: A good deal.

JACKIE: How lovely!

RICHARD COMES DOWN AND SITS ON FORM BELOW PIANO. THERE IS A PAUSE.

RICHARD: Spain is very beautiful.

JACKIE: Yes, I've always heard Spain was awfully nice.

PAUSE

RICHARD: Except for the bull-fights. No one who ever loved horses could enjoy a bull-fight.

JACKIE: Nor anyone who loved bulls either.

RICHARD: Exactly.

PAUSE

JACKIE: Italy's awfully nice, isn't it?

RICHARD: Oh yes, charming.

JACKIE: I've always wanted to go to Italy.

PAUSE.

At the end of the first act, the guests find themselves assembled for afternoon tea, but again the Blisses' refusal to participate in ritual politenesses makes it a devastating affair; scattered about on unsuitable seats in the hall, balancing cups and plates, they try to exchange pleasantries in the face of their hosts' indifference, but give up in discouragement; after two attempts, during which they find themselves uttering simultaneous banalities, the curtain comes down on an embarrassed pause.

The play is not simply about the Blisses' lack of conventional manners but about the manners they have made for themselves. Much of the discomfiture of the guests arises from the fact that there is a code of conduct in the house which they do not understand. Simon makes it clear at the start of the play that it is not a code for everybody. 'It's so silly of people to try and cultivate the artistic temperament', he remarks of an acquaintance. '*Au fond* she's just a normal, bouncing Englishwoman.' The Blisses are aware that they have talent and that it needs outlets for display. They adopt a variety of masks which they parade for the admiration of others. Judith, for instance, speaks of 'my Celebrated Actress glamour' as an entity which 'isn't me really'; she also recognises that certain masks are quite beyond her; despite her attempts to learn the names of the flowers and her determination in marching about with a trug and galoshes, she decides that 'I've tried terribly hard to be "landed gentry", but without any real success'. Role-play within the family provides them with a source of endless entertainment; they can launch spontaneously and with gusto into the second act curtain scene from Judith's great stage success *Love's Whirlwind* or become totally absorbed in a reading of David's new novel; this imbues their behaviour with an enormous vitality which partly offsets their ruthlessness. Role-play is also a cohesive force for the Blisses. Although they quarrel incessantly the situation is always resolved through spontaneous improvisation. As they squabble about whose guest will get the Japanese room and who will have the boat to go on the river, Judith takes charge; she launches into a speech of tender melancholy ('A change has come over my children of late . . .'), grabs Simon and Sorel and arranges them in suitable poses which they understand only too well are cues for a scene of family togetherness:

SIMON *COMES OVER TO HIS MOTHER*: Mother, what are we to do?
JUDITH *PULLS HIM DOWN ON HIS KNEES AND PLACES HIS HEAD ON HER RIGHT SHOULDER, SOREL'S HEAD ON HER LEFT. MAKES A CHARMING LITTLE MOTHERLY*

PICTURE: We must all be very, very kind to everyone!

SIMON: Now then, Mother, none of that!

JUDITH *AGGRIEVED*: I don't know what you mean, Simon.

SIMON: You were being beautiful and sad.

JUDITH: But I am beautiful and sad.

SIMON: You're not particularly beautiful, darling, and you never were.

JUDITH: Never mind; I made thousands think I was.

Judith neatly averts the quarrel and also focuses attention on herself, creating an atmosphere in which she can announce that she is returning to the stage – and does it without fooling anyone in the least. Etiquette, for the Blisses, is not to create polite and impenetrable fictions, but to create shared improvisations, fictions in which the polite guest should participate. Talented hosts need talented guests; if they end up with untalented ones, they reserve the right to show no mercy.

Coward opens the second act with a scene in which the guests' lack of role-playing talent is cruelly and comically exposed. The Blisses set up a game called 'Adverbs', allied to charades. Coward makes of this a highly entertaining comic set-piece; he explores the embarrassment of the well-mannered guest forced to assume falsely the spontaneity of a child; he doubles the embarrassment by the fact that the hosts all have some contact, through Judith, with the professional theatre and none of the guests do; and compounds it further by the Blisses' relentless criticism of their guests' performance. Judith eggs on the disintegration of the game with a piece of staggering rudeness, pronouncing 'I think, for the future, we'd better confine our efforts to social conversation and not attempt anything in the least intelligent.' This heavy irony is more than an insult, however: it is also a clear statement that the weekend is going to be played by Bliss rules whether the guests will or not. The game proves to have been a kind of initiation ceremony; for all its discomfort it is a good deal easier than the subsequent role-playing expected of the guests. In the second half of the play Coward takes a more complex look at the relationship between charm and good manners.

When *Hay Fever* opened in 1925 Coward, fresh from *The Vortex* and *Fallen Angels*, epitomised for much of his audience the 'younger generation knocking on the door of the dustbin'. With this in mind he left John Gielgud to play Nicky Lancaster in *The Vortex* on the first night of *Hay Fever* and came on at the final curtain to point out that 'this play at least, ladies and gentlemen, has been as clean as a whistle'. Clean it might be: certainly every embrace is interrupted and every burgeoning love-affair thwarted; but the second half of the play is nonetheless largely concerned with the uses that charm makes of sexual attraction and the strategies which conventional good manners employ to cope with it.

Certainly Judith's talent has no trouble in weaving a spell around Richard. She manipulates him expertly, first with a display of professional talent as she sings at the piano, then by the adoption of a carefully calculated persona:

RICHARD: I never realise how *dead* I am until I meet people like you. It's depressing, you know.
JUDITH: What nonsense! You're not a bit dead.
RICHARD: Do you always live here?
JUDITH: I'm going to, from now onwards. I intend to sink into a very beautiful old age. When the children marry, I shall wear a cap.

RICHARD *SMILING*: How absurd!

JUDITH: I don't mean a funny cap.

RICHARD: You're far too full of vitality to sink into anything.

JUDITH: It's entirely spurious vitality. If you troubled to look below the surface, you'd find a very wistful and weary spirit. I've been battling with life for a long time.

With a neat lie (she has every intention of going back to the stage) she makes herself appear to share Richard's peace-loving spirit; she also deftly calls attention to the age gap between them in order to make Richard himself deny it; and by a touch of wistfulness dissociates herself from the quarrelsome antics of 'Adverbs', instigated by her only minutes before. Richard, duly charmed, plays up as he is clearly expected to do and kisses her. It seems momentarily that host and guest have found some common territory of manners. Desire has its own set of 'good manners'; a little polite insincerity is usual.

Each of the guests makes this same mistake. Sandy Tyrrel finds himself muttering 'I believe I do love you, Sorrel'. Jackie finds Simon sympathetic, and Myra makes a deliberate attempt to captivate David, piling on the flattery with a trowel:

MYRA: . . . I'm a very determined woman, you know, and I made up my mind to meet you ages ago.

DAVID: That was charming of you. I'm not much to meet really.

MYRA: You see, I'd read *Broken Reeds*.

DAVID: Did you like it?

MYRA: Like it! I think it's one of the finest novels I've ever read.

DAVID: There now!

MYRA: How do you manage to know so much about women?

But for the Blisses, desire is subject to the same rules as their other kinds of behaviour. While, for the guests, flirtation involves a willing suspension of disbelief (flattery must be taken at face value, the casual kiss must have no long-term consequences while simultaneously disguising itself as a declaration of love) for the Blisses it involves *belief* in the value of the game for its own sake, in the pleasure of a cunningly constructed artifice. If the mask is to sustain its sexual glamour, it must first acknowledge itself. Sorel gently explodes Sandy's illusions: 'You kissed me because you were awfully nice and I was awfully nice and we both like kissing very much', she points out. David gives the more intelligent Myra a rougher time. He tells her firmly 'I write very bad novels . . . and you *know* I do, because you're an intelligent person.' He goes to the heart of the matter with embarrassing directness, asking 'Would you like me to make love to you?' Finally he explains the code by which he and the other Blisses live:

DAVID: . . . The only reason I've been so annoying is that I love to see things as they are first, and then pretend they're what they're not.

MYRA: Words. Masses and masses of words!

DAVID: They're great fun to play with.

MYRA: I'm glad you think so. Personally, they bore me stiff.

DAVID: Myra – don't be statuesque.

Judith's technique for dealing with the hypocrisies of flirtation is even more radical: pretending to accept them, she then proceeds to transmute them into a parody of the

Victorian *mores* that the twenties had already begun to erode; she opens up essentially private moments into team games for the family, in which their improvisatory talents can enjoy free play. Every interrupted embrace becomes a centre for wild eddies of theatricality, Judith herself always in the major role. Thus Richard's kiss becomes the cue for her to put on the mask of erring but fundamentally noble wife. 'David must be told – everything!' she tells the terrified Richard. Confronted by Sorel and Sandy kissing in the library, she becomes the older woman who renounces her lost love à la Lady Frederick; Sorel responds with delight:

JUDITH *STARTING TO ACT*: It's far from easy, at my time of life, to –

SOREL *PLAYING UP*: Mother – Mother – say you understand and forgive!

JUDITH: Understand! You forget, dear, I am a woman.

SOREL: I know you are, Mother. That's what makes it all so poignant.

The improvisations gain momentum: the second act brings them all to a boil as Judith discovers David and Myra and plays a series of variations on the role of wronged wife. Myra becomes left behind as Judith and David top each other's melodramatic excesses; and when a puzzled Richard enters assuming that the shouting is about him, that David has indeed been 'told – everything!' he provides the Blisses with a perfect cue to unite by inadvertently quoting from *Love's Whirlwind*:

RICHARD *WITH FORCED CALM*: What's happened? Is this a game?

JUDITH'S FACE GIVES A SLIGHT TWITCH;

*THEN, WITH A MEANING LOOK AT SIMON
AND SOREL, SHE ANSWERS HIM*
JUDITH *WITH SPIRIT*: Yes, and a game that must be
played to the finish! *SHE FLINGS BACK HER ARM
AND KNOCKS RICHARD UP STAGE.*
SIMON *GRASPING THE SITUATION*: Zara! What
does this mean?

The curtain falls as the whole family assume their roles in
the moth-eaten melodrama; Sorel raises her hand to strike
Simon and is warned by a fainting Judith 'Don't strike! He
is your father!!!'

The game is a way of excluding the non-talented from the
Blisses' circle; but it also makes a comment on the
assumptions on which they have tried to enter it; all guests,
except the dim Jackie, have come for the weekend
expecting to flirt, to put on the only mask in which they feel
comfortable. The Pinero-like scenes they find themselves
playing are a kind of nightmare in which all their masks are
taken seriously, and that by people who have already
demonstrated that, as Sorel puts it, 'We none of us mean
anything.' Coward allows us to enjoy the comedy of masks
to the full by refusing to take sides. The guests may be
treated badly, but they are also capable of selfishness
towards one another in their difficulties; the appalling
breakfast in the third act is the stage for various attempts to
secure the right to leave first and push others into staying so
that their departure will seem less rude. Our last sight of the
Blisses also shows their selfishness: a quarrel about the
geography of Paris as described in David's novel is halted
by the sound of the departing car, carrying off the people
with whom they have neglected to take breakfast. Judith's
comment is 'How very rude!'

Hay Fever is Coward's most exuberant play, his most

unqualified celebration of the sheer fun of mask-making and the way in which the dullest phrase like 'Is this a game?' can spark off a linguistic and gestural explosion. Of all his major comedies, it is also the only one which did not contain a part for himself, and the two facts are perhaps not unconnected. Although *Hay Fever* demands exceptional ensemble playing, it centres on Judith. Coward created the part for the forceful actress Marie Tempest, who was trying in the twenties to establish herself as a capable performer of contemporary plays; she was able to exploit her rich experience of working in plays not unlike *Love's Whirlwind*, imbuing the lively parodies with affection. Since then the role has, despite Judith's vagueness, always worked best with an actress of authority – Edith Evans played in the famous National revival directed by Coward. The distancing effect of writing the major role for someone other than himself allowed Coward to portray the lethal effect of charm from the outside only, and thus, perhaps, to celebrate it in a more uninhibited fashion. In his last major comedy, however, *Present Laughter* he created a figure with a more ambivalent relationship to his mask. 'Garry Essendine', he stated in a radio talk in 1972, 'is me', and the role is a potent mixture of self-exposure and self-celebration.

As in *Hay Fever*, we see a group of relatively conventional outsiders impinging upon a circle which makes its own manners. Once again, the central figure of that circle is a performer, both on and off the stage. However, we also see, in *Present Laughter*, some of the machinery which exists to service the performer's public face. Judith calls for, and gets, the moral and histrionic support of her family as she launches into the role of loving mother or betrayed wife, but her talent appears to flow of its own accord. Garry's is a commercial proposition; the 'family' which surrounds him is his staff, a collection of secretaries, managers and domestic servants not unlike Coward's own entourage in structure. They offer affection and support but are also determined to protect their investment. They discuss his looks (including the possibility of a toupée), his appointments, his finances and his potential as an actor, stamping frequently on his desire to play Peer Gynt; they also try to control his offstage charm and the consequences of it. 'Think what fun it would be to be *un*attractive for a minute or two', urges his ex-wife and still devoted scriptwriter, Liz.

If charm depends upon businesslike support, however, it also gives back, and not only in terms of a return on the original investment. It also recognises and brings out talent in others.

GARRY: . . . Twenty years ago Henry put all his money into *The Lost Cavalier*. And who played in it for eighteen months to capacity with extra matinees? I did. And who started his career as a producer in that play? Morris!

LIZ: I wish you'd stop asking questions and answering them yourself, it's making me giddy.

GARRY: Where would they have been without me? Where would Monica be now if I hadn't snatched her away from that sinister old aunt of hers and given her a job?

LIZ: With the sinister old aunt.

GARRY: And you! One of the most depressing melancholy actresses on the English stage. Where would you be if I hadn't forced you to give up acting and start writing?

LIZ: Regent's Park.

GARRY: Good God, I even had to marry you to do it.

Three outsiders attempt in different ways to fracture this

delicate symbiosis. Like the guests in *Hay Fever* they fail to understand the relationship between mask and performer, but the mistake they make is different. While Richard and the others do not grasp the impact of their amorous comings and goings on the play that is running perpetually in Judith's mind, the outsiders of *Present Laughter* treat Garry's attractiveness as a function of an individual; in fact it is the property of a group. Their desires are all different. Daphne, the debutante, wants a love affair; Roland Maule, the playwright, wants Garry to stop 'prostituting himself' in boulevard comedy and commit himself to the 'theatre of tomorrow' (ie, his plays); Joanna, the wife of Garry's business partner Henry, has a more sophisticated understanding of Garry's persona; she expects him to act, offstage as well as on; while she wants casual dalliance rather than deeply felt passion, she still puts her own desire ahead of the happiness of 'the firm'. All three, in fact, hold a Romantic conception of the artist as individual, and the play happily explodes the myth while celebrating the fact that, despite its function as a business investment, charm is a magical gift to the performer at the centre of that investment.

Garry's talent, unlike Judith's, does not flow freely from the play but always works towards a goal. Constantly, he charms his way to people's affections and then tries to charm his way out of them. Daphne, for instance, has spent the night before the opening curtain watching Garry in the role of disillusioned but tender Older Man, a role that his staff know well:

> DAPHNE: We talked for hours last night. He told me all about his early struggle.
>
> MONICA: Did he by any chance mention that Life was passing him by?

Garry's attempts to brush off Daphne also consist largely of a display of masks. He recites Shelley, he elaborates on the fragility and beauty of illusion and the glories of what might have been. Coward's stage directions have a touch of parody about them here: Garry dismisses her view of him as too melancholy 'LAUGHING BITTERLY', he asserts that he will always remember her 'WITH BEAUTIFUL SIMPLICITY'; they are, in fact, the stage directions with which Garry is clearly directing himself in his head.

With all his hangers-on, eventually Garry resorts to the most potent mask of all – the pretence that there is no pretence, that all masks are off:

> I'm always acting – watching myself go by – that's what's so horrible – I see myself all the time eating, drinking, loving, suffering – sometimes I think I'm going mad –

This technique never fails to charm. Daphne continues to haunt him, turning up incognito to an audition to recite Shelley back at him. Roland is subjected to a tirade about his play, which Garry considers 'a meaningless jumble of adolescent, pseudo intellectual poppycock', and it entrances him; drawn to Garry's energy, he too insists on hanging around.

Charm, in fact, permeates Garry's whole being. He uses it so instinctively that he cannot stop using it, for the cessation of charm becomes charming in itself. With Joanna, the most articulate and dangerous outsider, he even produces a third layer of the mask. She makes the admission that he is always acting into a springboard for a little male–female aggression:

> JOANNA: You're being conventionally odious but somehow it doesn't quite ring true. But then you never

do quite ring true, do you? I expect it's because you're an actor, they're always apt to be a bit papier maché.

GARRY: Just puppets, Joanna dear, creatures of tinsel and sawdust, how clever of you to have noticed it.

The aggression and its aftermath provokes Garry into his last and perhaps favourite pose, that of the honest voice crying in the wilderness; he rounds on Joanna's own mask:

You suddenly appear out of the night reeking with the lust of conquest, the whole atmosphere's quivering with it! You had your hair done this afternoon, didn't you? and your nails and probably your feet too! That's a new dress, isn't it? Those are new shoes! You've never worn those stockings before in your life! And your mind, even more expertly groomed to vanquish than your body. Every word, every phrase, every change of mood cunningly planned. Just the right amount of sex antagonism mixed with subtle flattery, just the right switch over, perfectly timed, from provocative implication to wistful diffidence. You want to know what I'm like, do you, under all the glittering veneer? Well this is it. This is what I'm really like – fundamentally honest!

Joanna's reply, 'Curtain!' is accurate; it also cements the basis of their subsequent love-making – they are going to play at honesty, discussing the emotional implications of a night together upon the rest of 'the firm' before dropping into free improvisation as Garry makes a love duet out of the names of London concert halls.

John Lahr sees Garry's charm as a dilemma identical with Coward's own. 'In the play Coward admits the artificiality of his persona only to make its charm triumphant. Underneath *Present Laughter*'s high spirits is a dilemma: a man who dissimulates so eagerly that he has

forgotten who he is.'[23] While this description may fit
Coward the playwright and actor, Garry at least has a
solution. His compulsion to attract may embroil him in
annoying situations: Roland, Daphne and Joanna all arrive
in the final act threatening to accompany him to Africa, and
Joanna vengefully insists on telling her husband that she
has spent the night with Garry. He is, however, entirely
capable of dealing with them all, by shutting up Roland and
Daphne in the spare room and the office and by some
straight talking to 'the firm' about their own love lives.
There is no suggestion that he is existentially threatened by
his own charm; in fact he contrasts the insecurities of the
others, their attitude to sex as an anodyne or a collector's
item or a security symbol, with his own awareness that
attractiveness is evanescent and the peace of mind that this
knowledge gives:

> To me the whole business is vastly over-rated. I enjoy it
> for what it's worth and fully intend to go on doing so for
> as long as anybody's interested and when the time comes
> that they're not I shall be perfectly content to settle down
> with an apple and a good book!

The real histrionics in this scene are reserved for matters of
business, for the problems of the forthcoming tour of
Africa and the choice of venues for his return performance.
Even *Peer Gynt* rears its head once more, and the fury of
Joanna as woman scorned pales into insignificance beside
Garry's tirade against the Forum theatre. As Garry tiptoes
offstage with Liz as the curtain falls, we are witnessing
more than a neat escape from his immediate problems. Liz
is the most powerful symbol of 'the firm' who look after the
Essendine mask. Garry has not lost his personality. He has,
rather, handed it over to others for safe keeping.

Joanna, the outsider, is vitriolic about his dependence on

his satellites. 'It's too dangerous for a little tinsel star to go twinkling off alone and unprotected,' she says sarcastically. but 'the firm' remains intact precisely because both they and Garry recognise the truth of this. The play contains episodes which come closer to French farce than anything else in Coward's *oeuvre*: but there is still a crucial difference. Garry's sense of self is never threatened, because every vicissitude prompts a therapeutic outburst, a monologue on anything from the state of the theatre to the prospect of a tour of 'what is admitted to be by everybody the most sinister continent there is': moreover, these outbursts are controlled, even fine-tuned, by the judicious comments of the firm'. 'It's a pity they're pulling down the Lyceum', says Henry acidly, and Garry switches off the *Angst* at once and has a drink. And when Joanna hides in the spare room from Henry and Morris, the action takes on the speed and energy of farce but the stakes which are being played for are different. No-one on stage has any interest in reputation or respectability; indeed the 'spare room' becomes a kind of running joke throughout the play and to 'lose a latch-key' and spend the night in it has a meaning perfectly clear to all. What is at risk, however, is the harmony of 'the firm.' Liz helps Joanna to hide while making it very clear that she will have to break with Garry:

> JOANNA: I suppose you're still in love with Garry yourself?
> LIZ: Not in the least, but even if I were it's entirely beside the point. I certainly love him. I love Henry and Morris too. We've all been devoted to one another for many years, and it would take more than you to break it up permanently. But I'm not taking any risks of you even upsetting it temporarily. You're going to do what I tell you.

JOANNA: And what if I don't?

LIZ: You'll be out, my dear, with all of us, for ever.

Charm may have its problems, in that it draws others into its net almost against its will; the mask may become a trap. But when charm is a business it can also create friendship; the common task of manipulating it brings 'the firm' together. Outsiders may be hurt by it or excluded from it, but it is no longer locked in the dilemma of Elyot and Amanda, who cannot bear either to be taken at face value or to be seen through. Paradoxically, this play which celebrates stardom and egoism also celebrates comradeship and values it more highly than individual erotic passion.

Garry was also Coward's last real 'whacking good part' until the afterword of *Suite in Three Keys*. He appeared in his own plays and those of others after *Present Laughter*, but its delayed London opening in 1943 was the last occasion on which he simultaneously celebrated himself and the commercial theatre which shaped him, in a role which seems specifically designed to allow the actor's own pleasure in theatricality to have fullest play. After this the 'theatre of tomorrow', which he had incarnated in the role of the appalling Roland and shut up in a cupboard, was to become too powerful to ignore and too certain of its own intellectual strength to fear this kind of ridicule. But with his five major comedies, Coward had established his own place in the theatrical order. As Robert Bolt pointed out in a reply to Coward's strictures on the New Wave, 'We are truly sorry our first effort at a vintage of our own should taste so nasty to a cultivated palate . . . But it can't be helped. We think that other bottle is quite, quite empty. It was Mr. Coward who had the last of it.'[24]

7
Afterword

The eighties saw a large number of revivals of Coward's major comedies, in the provinces and the West End. There has been an upsurge of interest in some other, lesser works – witness the expensively mounted *Cavalcade* at Chichester. A series of adaptations of Coward short stories ran in 1986 in a peak slot on television and as I write a glossy magazine is explaining the phrase 'Very Noel Coward':

> Pertaining to the Thirties. Very rarely used now to describe epigrams or situations, but frequently to describe blazers, white flannels, cigarette-holders, cocktail shakers etc, usually in the slightly mocking formula 'Oh, very Noel Coward.'[1]

Clearly, the name still signifies something. Many of the meanings attached to it are as misleading as the exotically wicked connotations with which the twenties insisted on festooning it. For some audiences it seems to be the cue for a Recession-inspired nostalgia for a wholly imaginary pre-war world where you could get change from a fiver after a night at the Ritz and always find good servants. 'Noel Coward' is the code for a blandly entertaining good night out. On the other hand the name can bring a glaze to the eyes of those reared in a newer theatrical mode: to my own students it signified simply bad and dated theatre, although when asked to perform in what they considered a Noel Coward style they came up with a whole variety of 'badness' ranging from Irvingnesque declamation to a strangulated 'naturalistic' delivery more suitable for sub-Rattigan. Coward's impact, it seems, is not in doubt, but his special contribution to the theatre is not always justly assessed or acknowledged.

He was not a great innovator in theatrical form, but he recharged the old forms with a new speed, trimming the elaborate plots of Maugham and his predecessors to the bone and relying on the play of mood to create dramatic shape; this in turn needed a new kind of dialogue and a new attitude to language. Compared to the plays current in Coward's childhood, his own dialogue was spare and allusive, needing more support from gesture and subtext. It was a process of stripping that was to continue in dramatic speech until Coward's own dialogue was to seem positively formal in comparison with newer writers like Pinter, who freely acknowledges his debt to him. He established, too, a new response on the part of characters to the language that they speak. With Maugham or Wilde characters are witty, epigrammatic and lively, but it is a fact they themselves take for granted. Coward's characters visibly enjoy their own cleverness; they make language into a game, irresistible even at moments of emotional crisis. Otto and Leo, for instance, faced with a life without Gilda, can still find time to ponder the absurdity of the word 'wimple'. This consciousness of language and its potential for play is one of Coward's lasting legacies to writers such as Pinter, Orton and Ann Jellicoe; Coward may not have liked all their work, but an episode such as the scene in Jellicoe's *The Knack* in which three people pretend that the bed is a piano and for five minutes utter no sounds but 'pling' and 'plong' is not substantially different from Elyot's attempt at small talk in *Private Lives*.

It seems unlikely now that Coward's five comedies will ever lose their popularity, but they have perhaps at present an especial value. As the social and political relationship between the sexes is undergoing traumatic changes, literary works which create strong images of those relationships past and present provide a touchstone for a new dialectic. As Marx put it (juggling with the term 'man' to signify both humankind and a particular gender):

> The most direct, natural and necessary relation of person to person is the *relation of man to woman*. In this *natural* relationship of the sexes man's relation to nature is immediately his relation to man, just as his relation to man is immediately his relation to nature – his own *natural* function. In this relationship therefore is *sensuously manifested*, reduced to an observable *fact*, the extent to which the human essence has become nature to man, or to which nature has to him become the human essence of man. From this relationship one can therefore judge man's whole level of development.[2]

One hopes that the latter half of the twentieth century might encompass all sexual relationships when setting up its criteria for judging the development of the race so far. And if any play depicting sexual relationships with life and style is vital to chart these relationships in the past, it is perhaps most true of comedy, and of the comedy of manners in particular. In plays like Coward's five we see reflected not only contemporary attitudes to relationships, but also the gap between what society would like those relationships to be and what they are. Coward's stylish lovers are at once an idealised image of what a relationship can be like and a warning.

If Coward had written no memorable plays at all, his image might serve the same purpose. In his own public persona he constructed something that was very much of his own time and place. It is impossible to imagine a Noel Coward who was not English; and equally impossible to envisage the possibility of his brand of stardom in an age in which the media have so much power. The kind of accessibility to the lives of its stars which the public now expects and gets would destroy the balance Coward maintained throughout his career; his relationship to the audience was partly that of an aloof and glamorous figure, partly that of an entertainer who did what was expected of him and altered the expected image of himself at his peril. He was, as few others even more accomplished have been, his own impresario and his own invention.

Chronology of Coward's Plays in Order of Composition

(with first production dates)

1918 *The Rat Trap* (1926).
1919 *I'll Leave it to You* (1920).
1920 *Barriers Down* (unproduced).
1921 *The Young Idea* (1922), *Sirocco* (1927), *The Better Half* (1922).
1922 *A Young Man's Fancy* (*unproduced*), *The Queen Was in the Parlour* (1926), *Bottles and Bones and Mild Oats* (*sketches*, 1922).
1923 *London Calling!* (1923), *The Vortex* (1924), *Fallen Angels* (1925), *Weatherwise* (*sketch*, 1932).
1924 *Hay Fever* (1925), *Easy Virtue* (New York 1925, London 1926).
1925 *On With the Dance* (1925).
1926 *Semi-Monde* (1977), *This Was a Man* (New York 1926), *The Marquise* (1927).
1927 *Pretty Prattle* (*sketch*, 1927), *Home Chat* (1927).
1928 *This Year of Grace!* (1928), *Concerto* (unproduced screenplay).
1929 *Bitter-Sweet* (1929).
1930 *Private Lives* (1930), *Post Mortem* (1944, POW production), *Some Other Private Lives* (*sketch*, 1930).
1931 *Cavalcade* (1931).

Chronology

1932 *Design for Living* (New York 1933, London 1939), *Words and Music* (1932).
1933 *Conversation Piece* (1934).
1934 *Point Valaine* (1934).
1935 *Tonight at 8.30* (ten plays, 1935).
1937 *Operette* (1938).
1939 *Present Laughter* (1942), *This Happy Breed* (1942).
1940 *Time Remembered* (unproduced).
1941 *Blithe Spirit* (1941), Screenplay for *In Which We Serve* (1942).
1945 *Sigh No More* (1945), *Pacific 1860* (1946).
1946 *Peace in Our Time* (1947).
1947 *Long Island Sound* (unproduced).
1949 *South Sea Bubble* (1956), *Ace of Clubs* (1950).
1950 *Relative Values* (1951).
1951 *Quadrille* (1952).
1954 *Nude with Violin* (1956).
1956 *Volcano* (unproduced).
1958 *Look after Lulu!* (adaptation of Feydeau's *Occupe-toi d'Amelie*, 1959).
1959 *Waiting in the Wings* (1960).
1961 *Sail away* (1961, London 1962).
1965 *Suite in Three Keys* (1966).

(This list does not include adaptations for the screen of his own works, non-dramatic verse, or prose or songs not collected in revues.)

References

1. The Mask

1. *Play Parade*, Vol. I, Heinemann 1934, p. x.
2. *Play Parade*, Vol. V, Heinemann 1958, p. xxxii.
3. Cole Lesley, *The Life of Noel Coward*, Jonathan Cape 1976, p. 57.
4. Rose Snider, *Satire in the Comedies of Congreve, Sheridan, Wilde and Coward*, Phaeton Press, New York, 1937, p. 116.
5. *New York Times*, 28 December 1969.
6. Cecil Beaton, *Self Portrait with Friends*, Weidenfeld and Nicholson 1979, pp. 11–12.
7. *Sunday Chronicle*, 26 April 1925.
8. *Future Indefinite*, Heinemann 1954, p. 51.
9. John Lahr, *Coward the Playwright*, Methuen 1982, p. 5.
10. Walter Benjamin, *Illuminations*, Fontana 1970, pp. 232–3.
11. *Present Indicative*, Heinemann 1937, pp. 200–1.
12. Cyril Connolly, *The Dandy*, in *The Evening Colonnade*, David Bruce and Watson 1973, p. 167.

2. Society's Hero

1. *The Oxford Book of 20th Century Verse*, Ed. Larkin, OUP 1973, p. 320.

References

1a. *The Times*, 27 November 1924.

2. Quoted in Richard Findlater, *Banned! A Study of Theatrical Censorship in Britain*, Macgibbon and Kee 1967, p. 77.

3. Foreword, Mander and Mitchenson, *Musical Comedy*, Davies, 1969.

4. *How I Write my Songs*, reprinted *Noel Coward and His Friends* ed. Lesley, Payn and Morley, Weidenfeld and Nicolson, 1979, p. 67.

5. Ivor Brown, *The Rise and Fall of the Matinee Idol*, ed. Curtis, New English Library 1976, p. 35.

6. Quoted Cole Lesley, *The Life of Noel Coward*, Cape 1976, p. 434.

7. Mander and Mitchenson, *A Theatrical Companion to Coward*, Rockliff 1957, p. 145.

8. *Present Indicative*, Heinemann 1937, p. 121.

9. *Play Parade II*, Heinemann 1939, p. ix.

10. Wilfred Owen, *Poems*, Chatto and Windus, 1920. Preface.

11. Alan Jenkins, *The Twenties*, Heinemann 1974, p. 5.

12. Owen, op. cit., *The Parable of the Old Man and the Young*, p. 57.

13. Evelyn Waugh, *Vile Bodies*, Eyre Methuen 1961, p. 129.

14. Quoted Margaretson, *The Long Party*, Saxon House, Farnborough, 1974, p. 52.

15. James Agate, *Saturday Review*, 17 February 1923.

16. *Play Parade I*, Heinemann 1934, p. xi.

17. *The Author's Reply to his Critics*, Introduction to *Three Plays*, Benn, 1925, p. ix.

18. Quoted Charles Castle, *Noel*, W. H. Allen 1974, p. 65.

19. St. John Irvine, *Observer*, 27 November 1927.

20. *Play Parade II*, Heinmann 1939, p. ix.

21. *New York Times*, 8 December 1925.

22. John Russell Taylor, *The Rise and Fall of the Well-Made Play*, Methuen 1967, p. 139.

3. Consider the Audience . . .

1. Emlyn Williams, Foreword, *The Turbulent Thirties*, Mander and Mitchenson, Macdonald 1960, p. 9.

2. Eagleton, *Exiles and Emigrés*, Chatto and Windus 1970, p. 73.

3. Quoted in Parker, *The Story and the Song*, Elm Tree Books 1979, p. 82.

4. Mander and Mitchenson, *Theatrical Companion to Coward*, op. cit., p. 143.

5. *Play Pictorial*, vol. lv, no. 330.

6. *Sketch*, 30 March 1938.

7. *Present Indicative*, p. 304.

8. *Present Indicative*, p. 401.

9. Rene Cutforth, *Later Than We Thought*, David and Charles 1976, p. 34.

10. Mander and Mitchenson, *Theatrical Companion to Coward*, op. cit., p. 195.

11. *Play Parade IV*, Heinemann 1954, p. x.

12. Ivor Brown, *Observer*, 12 January 1936.

13. Janet Flanner ('Gênet') *London Was Yesterday*, Michael Joseph 1970, p. 140.

14. *Sunday Times*, 15 January 1961.

15. *Present Indicative*, p. 117.

16. Sellars and Yeatman, *1066 and All That*, Methuen 1930, p. vii.

17. Quoted Sheridan Morley, *A Talent to Amuse*, Penguin 1974, pp. 184–5.

18. *Daily Telegraph*, 14 October 1931.

19. *Play Parade I*, Heinemann 1934, p. x.

20. *Present Indicative*, p. 270.

21. *Documentary News Letter*, Vol. I, 1944.

4.   'I've Had to Formulate a Creed . . .'

1. William Marchant, *The Privilege of his Company*, Weidenfeld and Nicholson 1975, p. 19.

2. *The Noel Coward Diaries*, ed. Payn and Morley, Weidenfeld and Nicholson 1982, p. 36, 26 July 1945.

3. *Diaries*, p. 179, 25 October–1 November 1951.

4. *Diaries*, p. 448, 11 September 1960.

5. Kenneth Tynan, *Tynan on Theatre*, Pelican 1964, p. 31.

6. John Whiting, *Coward Cruising, The London Magazine*, vol. 2 no. 5 p. 64.

7. *John O' London's Weekly*, 14 December 1951.

8. *Diaries*, p. 454, 16 December 1960.

9. *Diaries*, p. 409, 5 May 1959.

10. *Diaries*, p. 380, 25 May 1958.

11. John Raymond, *Play, Orchestra, Play, New Statesman* vol. LIV 25 October 1958.

12. Quoted *Noel Coward and his Friends*, ed. Payn and Morley, Weidenfeld and Nicolson 1979, p. 178.

13. *The Scratch and Mumble School, Sunday Times*, 22 January 1961.

14. *These Old-fashioned Revolutionaries, Sunday Times*, 15 January 1961.

15. *Sunday Times*, 22 January 1961.

16. *Sunday Times*, 22 January 1961.

References

17. *Collected Short Stories*, Methuen 1962, p. 483.
18. *Collected Short Stories*, p. 429.
19. *Daily Mail*, 8 September 1960.
20. *Daily Express*, 8 September 1960.
21. *Sunday Times*, 11 September 1960.
22. *Diaries*, p. 447. 11 September 1960.
23. *Diaries*, p. 497, 19 February 1962.
24. John Whiting, *Coward Cruising*.
25. Quoted Morley, *A Talent to Amuse*, p. 367.
26. *Diaries*, p. 679, 31 December 1969, the final entry.
27. *Diaries*, p. 512, 28 August 1962.
28. John Russell Taylor, *The Rise and Fall of the Well-made Play*, Methuen 1967, p. 144.
29. *Diaries*, p. 601, 23 June 1965.
30. *Diaries*, p. 452, 11 November 1960.
31. E.g., *The Times*, 15 April 1966.
32. Lahr, *Coward the Playwright*, p. 159.
33. Quoted Lahr, *Coward the Playwright*, p. 159.
34. D. A. N. Jones, *New Statesman*, vol. 71. p. 623, 26 April 1966.
35. *New Statesman*, 26 April 1966.

5. Mainly about Style

1. Kenneth Tynan, *Tynan on Theatre*, Pelican 1964, p. 288.
2. Terence Rattigan, *Noel Coward: An Appreciation of his work in the Theatre*, Preface, Mander and Mitchenson, *Theatrical Companion to Coward*, Rockliff 1957, p. 6.
3. Quoted Morley, *A Talent to Amuse*, Penguin 1974, p. 362.
4. Coward interviewed by Walter Harris on *Talking About Theatre*, Decca PLP 1138.
5. Tynan, *Some Notes on Stage Sexuality*, op. cit., p. 325.
6. *Noel Coward talks to Robert Muller*, Harper's Bazaar, August 1960.
7. *Play Parade I*, Heinemann 1934.
8. Christopher Isherwood, *The World in the Evening*, Methuen 1954.
9. Mark Booth, *Camp*, Quartet 1983, p. 17.
10. Quoted John Lahr, *Prick Up Your Ears*, Penguin 1980, p. 127.
11. Susan Sontag, *Against Interpretation*, Eyre and Spottiswoode 1967, p. 286.
12. John Lahr, *Coward the Playwright*, Methuen 1982, p. 5.
13. *Present Indicative*, Heinemann 1937, p. 373.
14. William Marchant, *The Privilege of his Company*, Weidenfeld and Nicolson 1975, p. 137.

15. Kenneth Tynan, *Tynan on Theatre*, p. 287.

16. Noel Coward, *A Withered Nosegay*, 1922, reprinted Methuen 1984, p. 104.

17. Laurence Olivier, *Confessions of an Actor*, Coronet 1984, p. 70.

18. *Diaries*, p. 581, 11 November 1964.

19. John Russell Taylor, *The Rise and Fall of the Well Made Play*, Methuen 1967, p. 140.

20. Quoted Kenneth Muir, *The Comedy of Manners*, Hutchinson 1970, p. 23.

21. George Meredeth, *On the Idea of Comedy*, Collected Works vol. xxxii, Constable and Co. 1898, p. 46.

22. Andrew Britton, *Comedy and Male Desire*, Tyneside Cinema Publications, Newcastle, 1983.

23. Roland Barthes, *Barthes on Barthes*, Tr. Howard, Macmillan 1977, p. 62.

6. Five Comedies

1. *Not Yet the Dodo and Other Verses*, Heinemann 1967, p. 34.

2. Graves and Hodge, *The Long Weekend*, Four Square 1961, p. 143.

3. Sheridan Morley, *A Talent to Amuse*, Penguin 1974, p. 388.

4. Cole Lesley, *The Life of Noel Coward*, Jonathan Cape 1976, p. 139.

5. *Present Indicative*, Heinemann 1937, p. 393.

6. *Present Indicative*, p. 395.

7. Sheridan Morley, *Gertrude Lawrence*, Weidenfeld and Nicolson 1981, p. 101.

8. *New Statesman*, vol. 36, 11 December 1930.

9. *Weekend Review*, 4 October 1930.

10. *Play Parade I*, Heinemann 1934, p. xvii.

11. *Observer*, 29 January 1939.

12. *Observer*, 29 January 1939.

13. John Lahr, *Coward the Playwright*, Methuen 1982, p. 85.

14. John Lahr, *Coward the Playwright*, p. 82.

15. *Present Indicative*, pp. 158–9.

16. Maurice Zolotow, *Stagestruck*, Heinemann 1965, p. 132.

17. O'Neill, *Strange Interlude*, Jonathan Cape 1928, p. 112.

18. *The Times*, 26 January 1939.

19. Sheridan Morley, *Review Copies*, Robson 1974, p. 220.

20. *The Noel Coward Diaries*, Payn and Morley, Weidenfeld and Nicolson 1982, p. 6, April 1941.

21. Gareth Lloyd Evans, *The Language of Modern Drama*, Dent 1977, p. 29.

References

22. Keith Thomas, *Religion and the Decline of Magic*, Penguin 1973, p. 717.
23. Lahr, *Coward the Playwright*, p. 32.
24. *Sunday Times*, 29 January 1961.

7. Afterword

1. *Cosmopolitan*, November 1985.
2. Marx, *Economic and Philosophical Manuscripts*, Moscow 1844, p. 101.

Bibliography

I. Collected plays

Play Parade I (*Cavalcade, Design for Living, Bitter-Sweet, Private Lives, Hay Fever, The Vortex, Post Mortem*), (Heinemann 1934).

Play Parade II (*This Year of Grace!*, Words and Music, *Operette, Conversation Piece, Easy Virtue, Fallen Angels*), (Heinemann 1939).

Play Parade III (*The Queen was in the Parlour, I'll Never Leave You, Sirocco, The Young Idea, The Rat Trap, This Was a Man, Home Chat, The Marquise*), (Heinemann 1950).

Play Parade IV (*Tonight at 8.30, Present Laughter, This Happy Breed*), (Heinemann 1954).

Play Parade V (*Blithe Spirit, Peace in Our Time, Quadrille, Relative Values, Pacific 1860*), (Heinemann 1958).

Play Parade VI (*Point Valaine, Ace of Clubs, South Sea Bubble, Nude with Violin, Waiting in the Wings*), (Heinemann 1962).

Eyre Methuen *Master Playwrights* collection in five volumes contains:

Plays One: *Hay Fever, The Vortex, Fallen Angels, Easy Virtue.*

Plays Two: *Private Lives, Bitter-Sweet, The Marquise, Post-Mortem.*

Plays Three: *Design for Living, Cavalcade, Conversation Piece, Tonight at 8.30 I.*

Plays Four: *Tonight at 8.30 II, Blithe Spirit, Present Laughter, This Happy Breed.*

Plays Five: *Relative Values, Waiting in the Wings, Look After Lulu, Suite in Three Keys*, ed. Mander and Mitchenson (Eyre Methuen 1979).

Bibliography

II. Other work by Noel Coward

Present Indicative (Heinemann 1937), and *Future Indefinite* (Heinemann 1954).

The Noel Coward Diaries, ed. Payn and Morley, (Weidenfeld and Nicolson 1982).

Collected Short Stories (Methuen 1983).

Pomp and Circumstance (novel, Methuen 1983).

The Lyrics of Noel Coward (Methuen 1983).

Not Yet the Dodo and Other Verses (Heinemann 1967).

A Withered Nosegay: Three Cod Pieces (Methuen 1984).

III. Books about Noel Coward

The best biographical accounts are *The Life of Noel Coward* by Cole Lesley, Coward's secretary and companion (Jonathan Cape 1976), and Sheridan Morley's *A Talent to Amuse* (Penguin 1974).

Additional useful photographic material can be found in *Noel* by Charles Castle (W. H. Allen 1972) and *Noel Coward and his Friends*, ed. Lesley, Payn and Morley (Weidenfeld and Nicolson 1979).

The most valuable reference book is Raymond Mander and Joe Mitchenson's *Theatrical Companion to Coward* (Rockliff 1957), indispensable to any study of Coward.

There is, unfortunately a considerable lack of good critical books on Coward; there are passing references in most books on modern theatre and some early studies of his work, but few detailed critical studies of the entire *oeuvre*. Any book on Coward at present will therefore, inevitably, incur a great debt to the work of John Lahr, whose study *Coward the Playwright* (Methuen 1982) is the latest and the best to put forward a coherent thesis about Coward's work.

Index

Index

Index

Index